X-MEN
FAIRY TALES

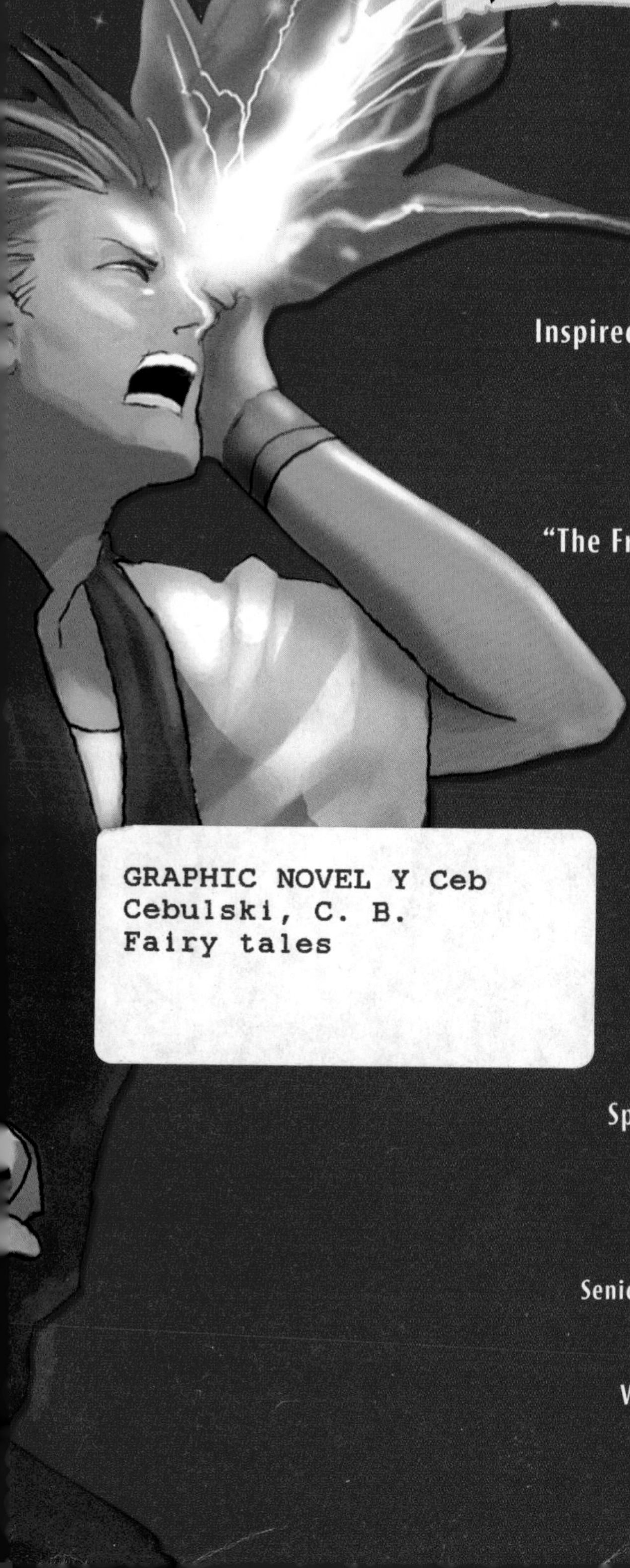

Writer: C.B. Cebulski

The Peach-Boy
Cover and Art: Sana Takeda
Inspired by the Japanese fairy tale "Momotaro"

Faith in Friends
Cover and Art: Kyle Baker
Inspired by the African fairy tale
"The Friendship of the Tortoise and the Eagle"

Restless Souls
Cover and Art: Kei Kobayashi
Colors: Guru eFX
Cover Art: Claire Wendling

To Die in Dreams
Artist: Bill Sienkiewicz
Colors: Guru eFX

Letters: Dave Sharpe
Consulting Editor: Mark Paniccia
Editor: Nathan Cosby
Special thanks to MacKenzie Cadenhead

Collection Editor: Jennifer Grünwald
Assistant Editor: Michael Short
Associate Editor: Mark D. Beazley
Senior Editor, Special Projects: Jeff Youngquist
Vice President of Sales: David Gabriel
Book Designer: Ryan Lewis
Vice President of Creative: Tom Marvelli

Editor in Chief: Joe Quesada
Publisher: Dan Buckley

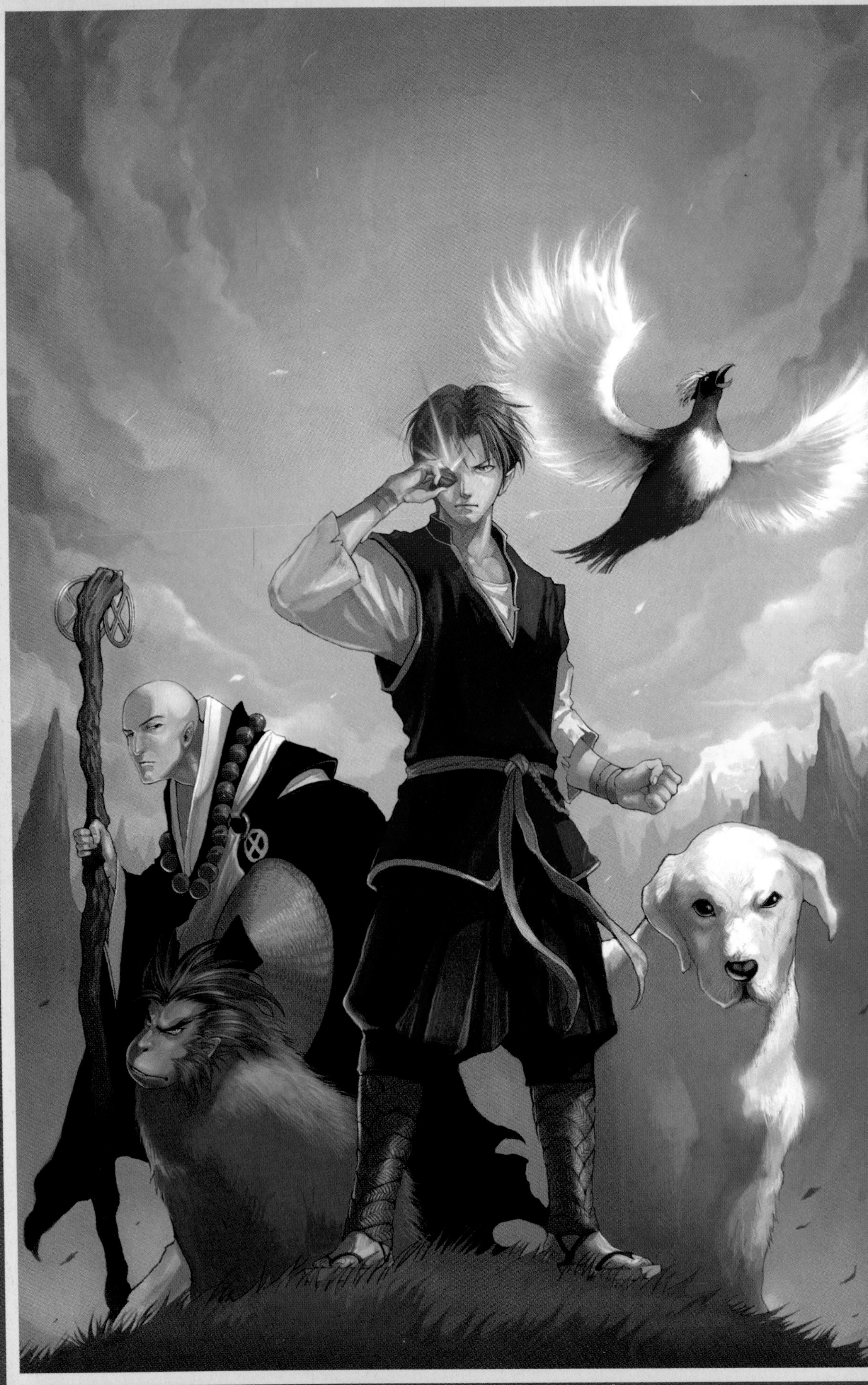

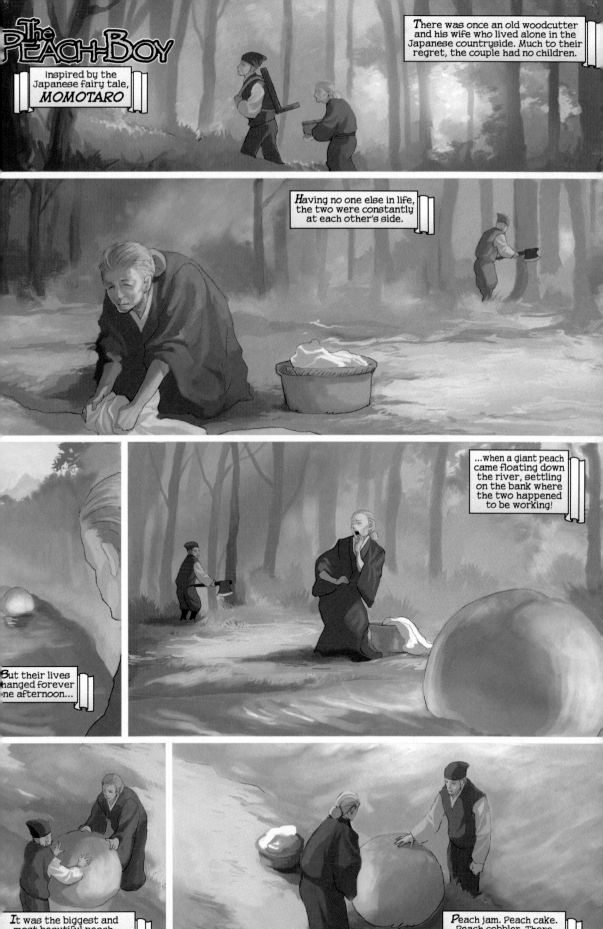

The PEACH-BOY

Inspired by the Japanese fairy tale, MOMOTARO

There was once an old woodcutter and his wife who lived alone in the Japanese countryside. Much to their regret, the couple had no children.

Having no one else in life, the two were constantly at each other's side.

...when a giant peach came floating down the river, settling on the bank where the two happened to be working!

But their lives changed forever one afternoon...

It was the biggest and most beautiful peach they had ever seen and they decided to take it home.

Peach jam. Peach cake. Peach cobbler. There would be enough dessert for a month!

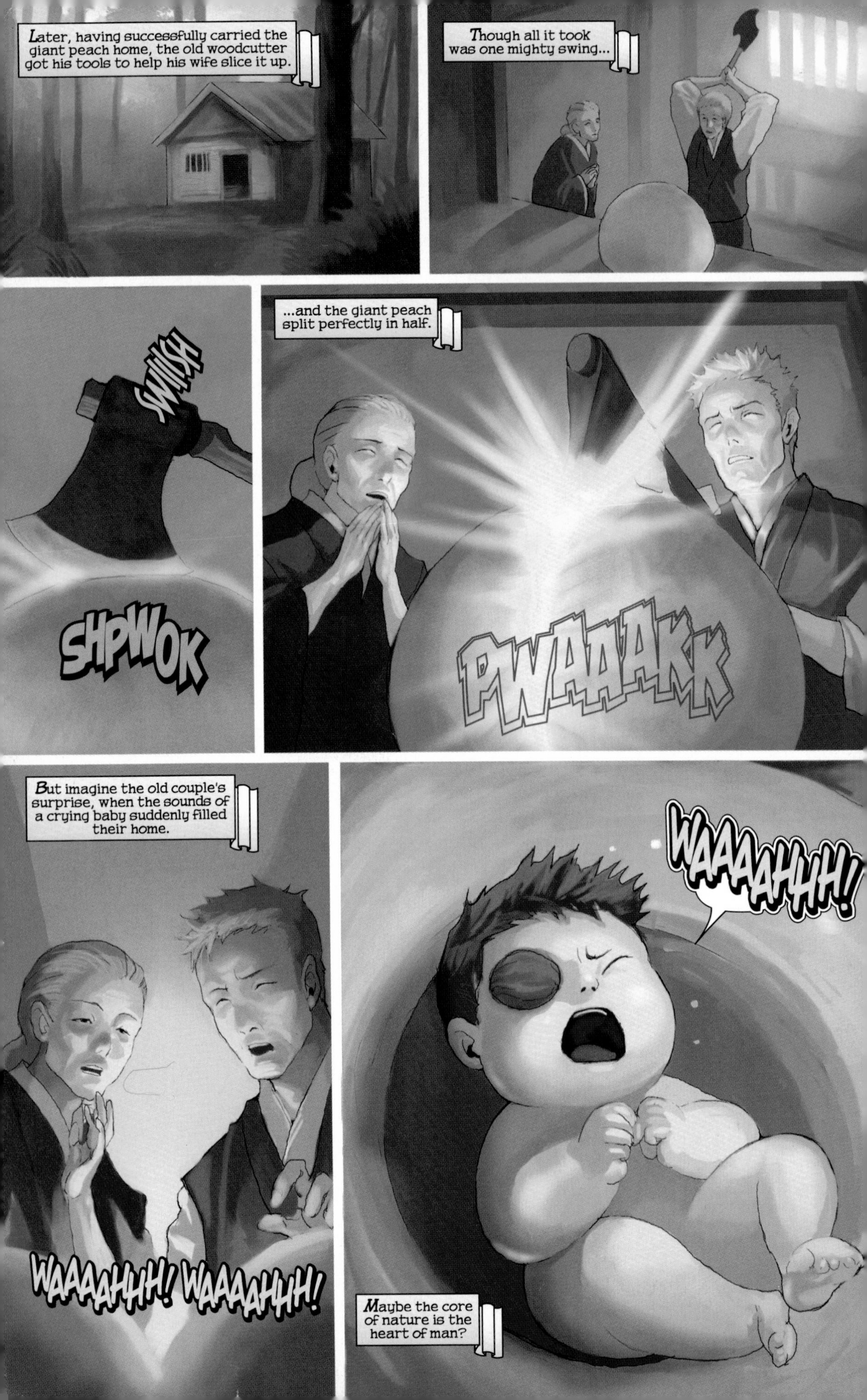

Later, having successfully carried the giant peach home, the old woodcutter got his tools to help his wife slice it up.
Though all it took was one mighty swing...
SWIISH
SHPWOK
...and the giant peach split perfectly in half.
PWAAAKK
But imagine the old couple's surprise, when the sounds of a crying baby suddenly filled their home.
WAAAAHHH! WAAAAHHH!
WAAAAHHH!
Maybe the core of nature is the heart of man?

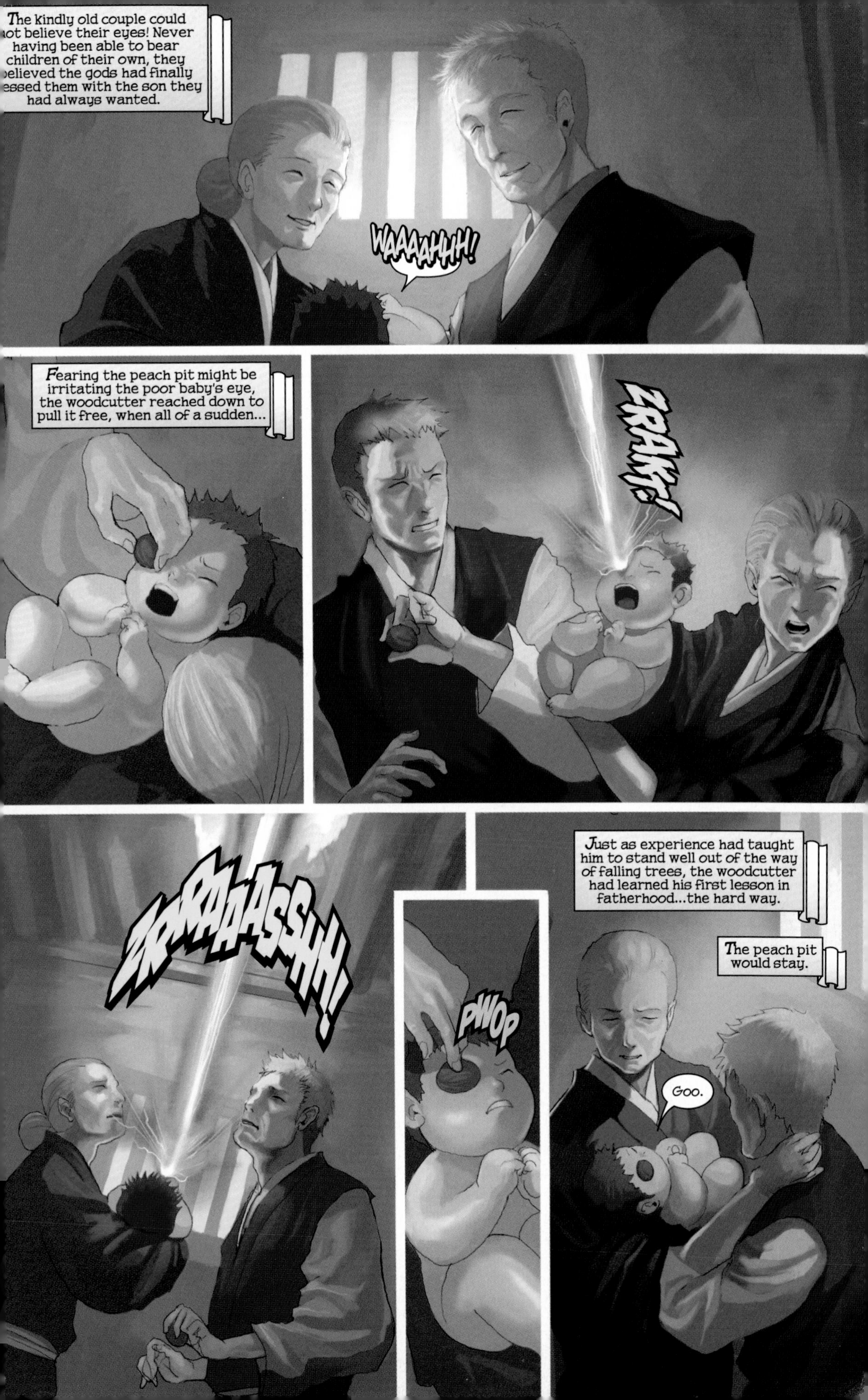
The kindly old couple could not believe their eyes! Never having been able to bear children of their own, they believed the gods had finally blessed them with the son they had always wanted.
WAAAAHHH!
Fearing the peach pit might be irritating the poor baby's eye, the woodcutter reached down to pull it free, when all of a sudden...
ZRAK!
ZRRAAAASSHH!
PWOP
Just as experience had taught him to stand well out of the way of falling trees, the woodcutter had learned his first lesson in fatherhood...the hard way.
The peach pit would stay.
Goo.

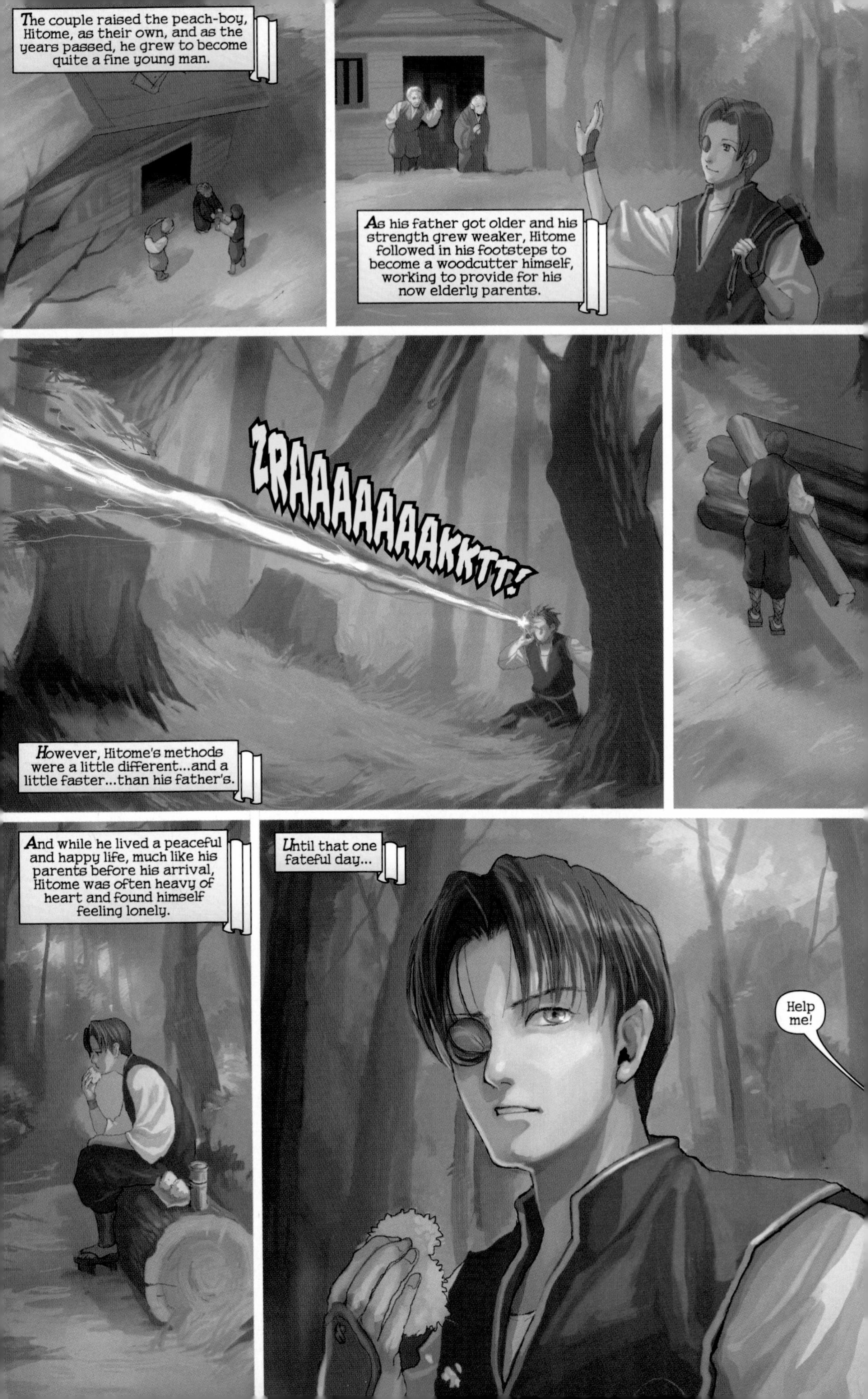
The couple raised the peach-boy, Hitome, as their own, and as the years passed, he grew to become quite a fine young man.
As his father got older and his strength grew weaker, Hitome followed in his footsteps to become a woodcutter himself, working to provide for his now elderly parents.
ZRAAAAAAAKKTT!
However, Hitome's methods were a little different...and a little faster...than his father's.
And while he lived a peaceful and happy life, much like his parents before his arrival, Hitome was often heavy of heart and found himself feeling lonely.
Until that one fateful day...
Help me!

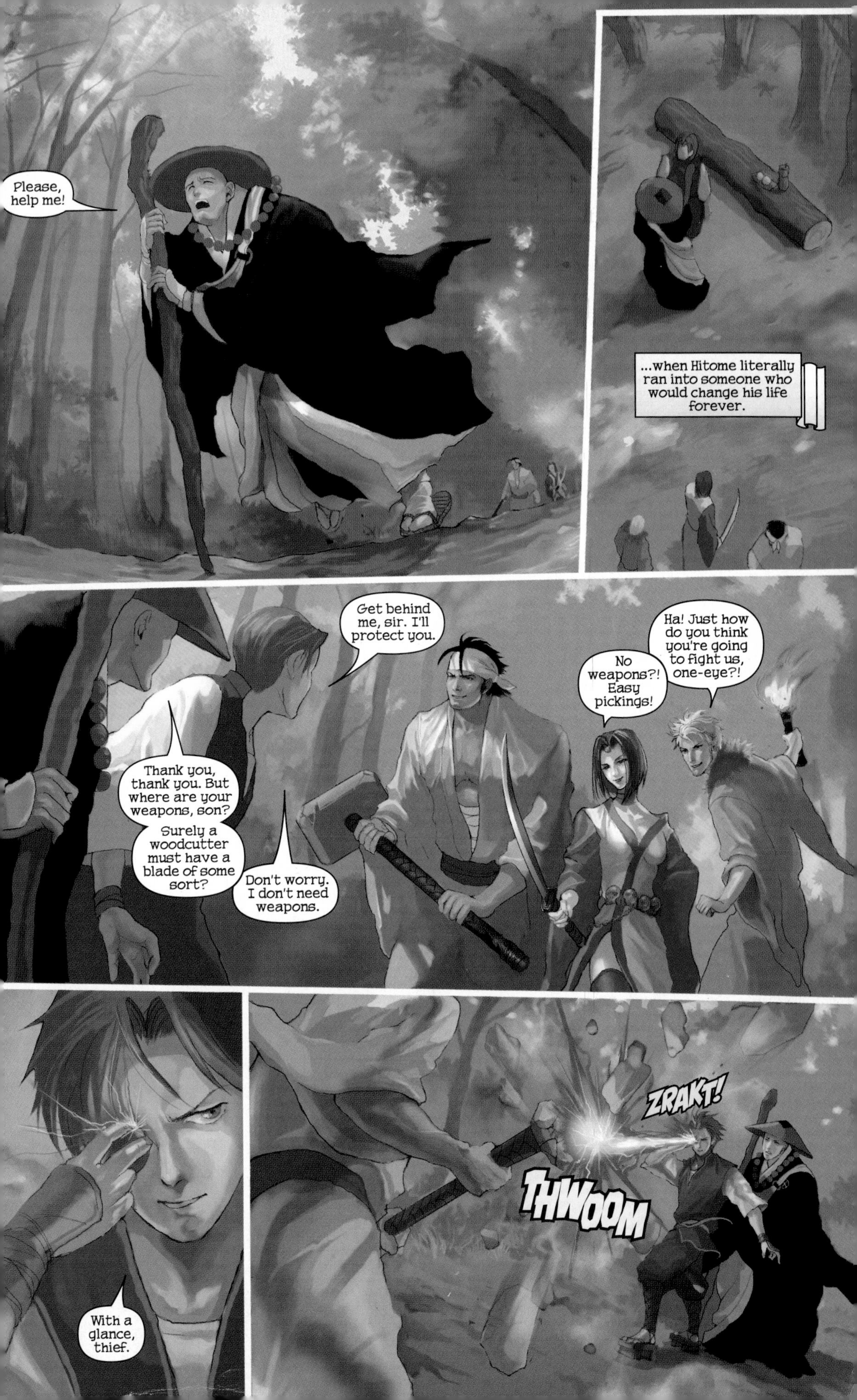
Please, help me!
...when Hitome literally ran into someone who would change his life forever.
Get behind me, sir. I'll protect you.
Thank you, thank you. But where are your weapons, son?
Surely a woodcutter must have a blade of some sort?
Don't worry. I don't need weapons.
No weapons?! Easy pickings!
Ha! Just how do you think you're going to fight us, one-eye?!
With a glance, thief.
ZRAKT!
THWOOM

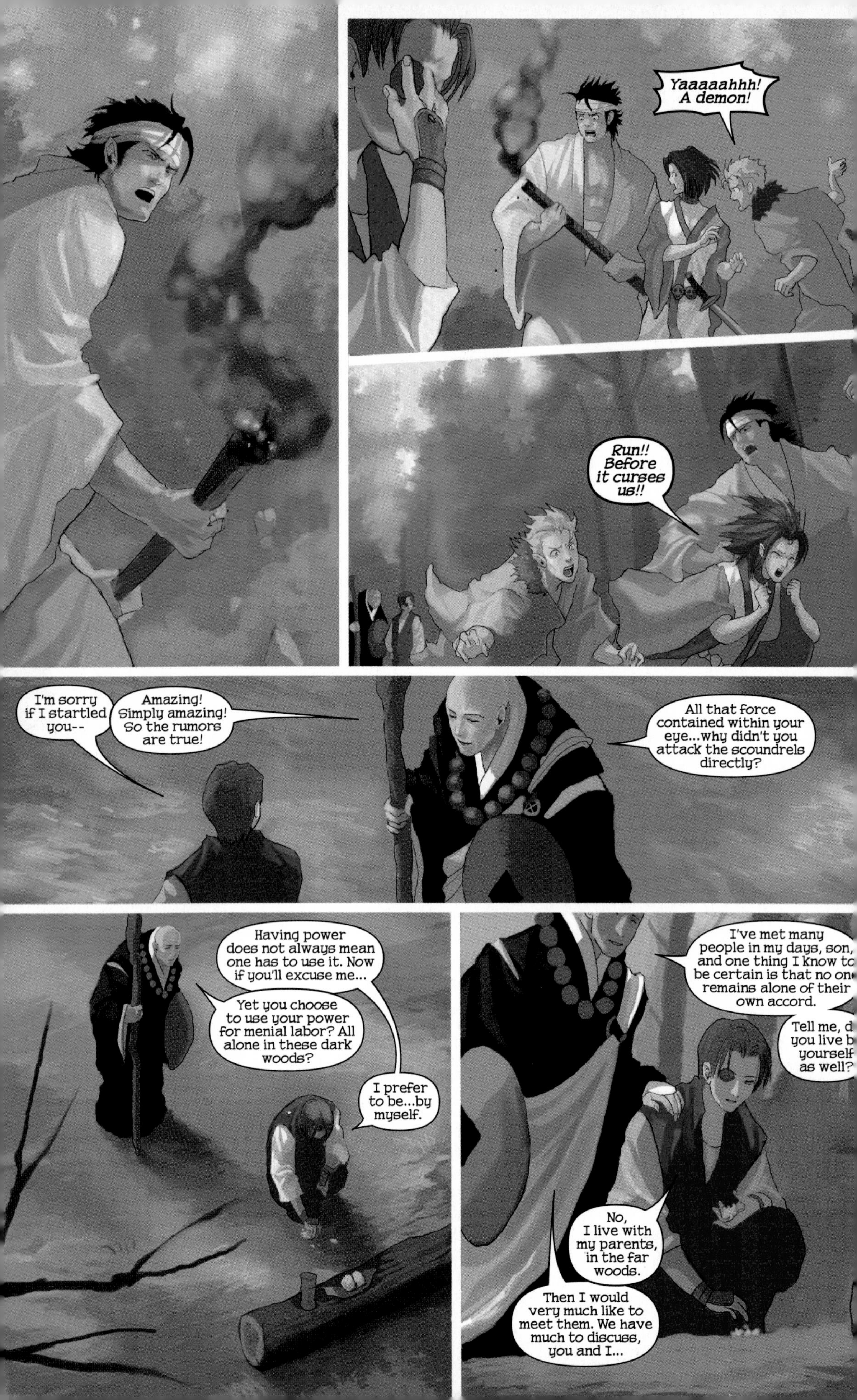
Yaaaaahhh! A demon!
Run!! Before it curses us!!
I'm sorry if I startled you--
Amazing! Simply amazing! So the rumors are true!
All that force contained within your eye...why didn't you attack the scoundrels directly?
Having power does not always mean one has to use it. Now if you'll excuse me...
Yet you choose to use your power for menial labor? All alone in these dark woods?
I prefer to be...by myself.
I've met many people in my days, son, and one thing I know to be certain is that no one remains alone of their own accord.
Tell me, do you live by yourself as well?
No, I live with my parents, in the far woods.
Then I would very much like to meet them. We have much to discuss, you and I...

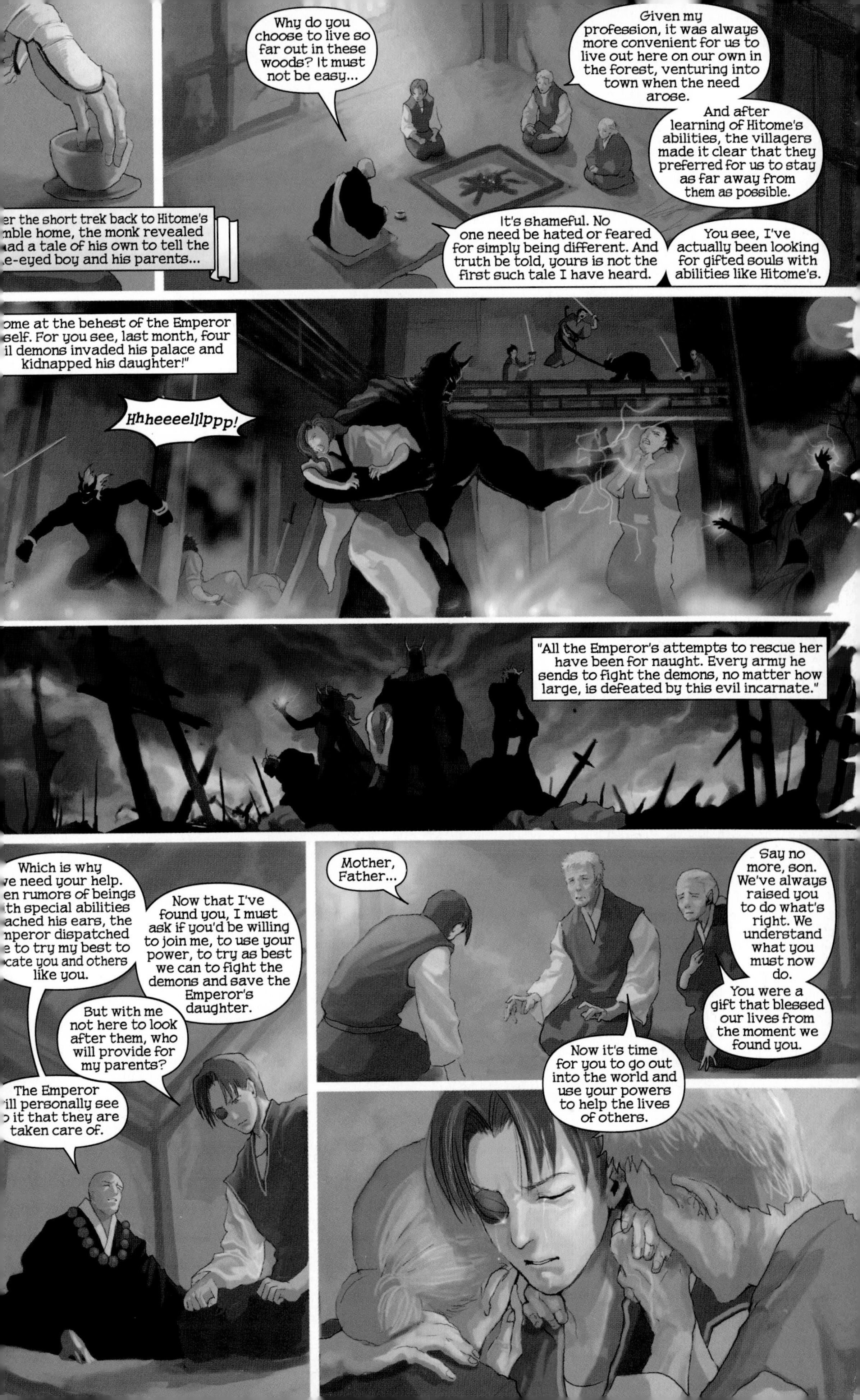

er the short trek back to Hitome's mble home, the monk revealed ad a tale of his own to tell the e-eyed boy and his parents...
Why do you choose to live so far out in these woods? It must not be easy...
Given my profession, it was always more convenient for us to live out here on our own in the forest, venturing into town when the need arose.
And after learning of Hitome's abilities, the villagers made it clear that they preferred for us to stay as far away from them as possible.
It's shameful. No one need be hated or feared for simply being different. And truth be told, yours is not the first such tale I have heard.
You see, I've actually been looking for gifted souls with abilities like Hitome's.
ome at the behest of the Emperor self. For you see, last month, four il demons invaded his palace and kidnapped his daughter!"
Hhheeeelllppp!
"All the Emperor's attempts to rescue her have been for naught. Every army he sends to fight the demons, no matter how large, is defeated by this evil incarnate."
Which is why ve need your help. en rumors of beings th special abilities ached his ears, the nperor dispatched e to try my best to cate you and others like you.
Now that I've found you, I must ask if you'd be willing to join me, to use your power, to try as best we can to fight the demons and save the Emperor's daughter.
But with me not here to look after them, who will provide for my parents?
The Emperor ill personally see o it that they are taken care of.
Mother, Father...
Say no more, son. We've always raised you to do what's right. We understand what you must now do.
You were a gift that blessed our lives from the moment we found you.
Now it's time for you to go out into the world and use your powers to help the lives of others.

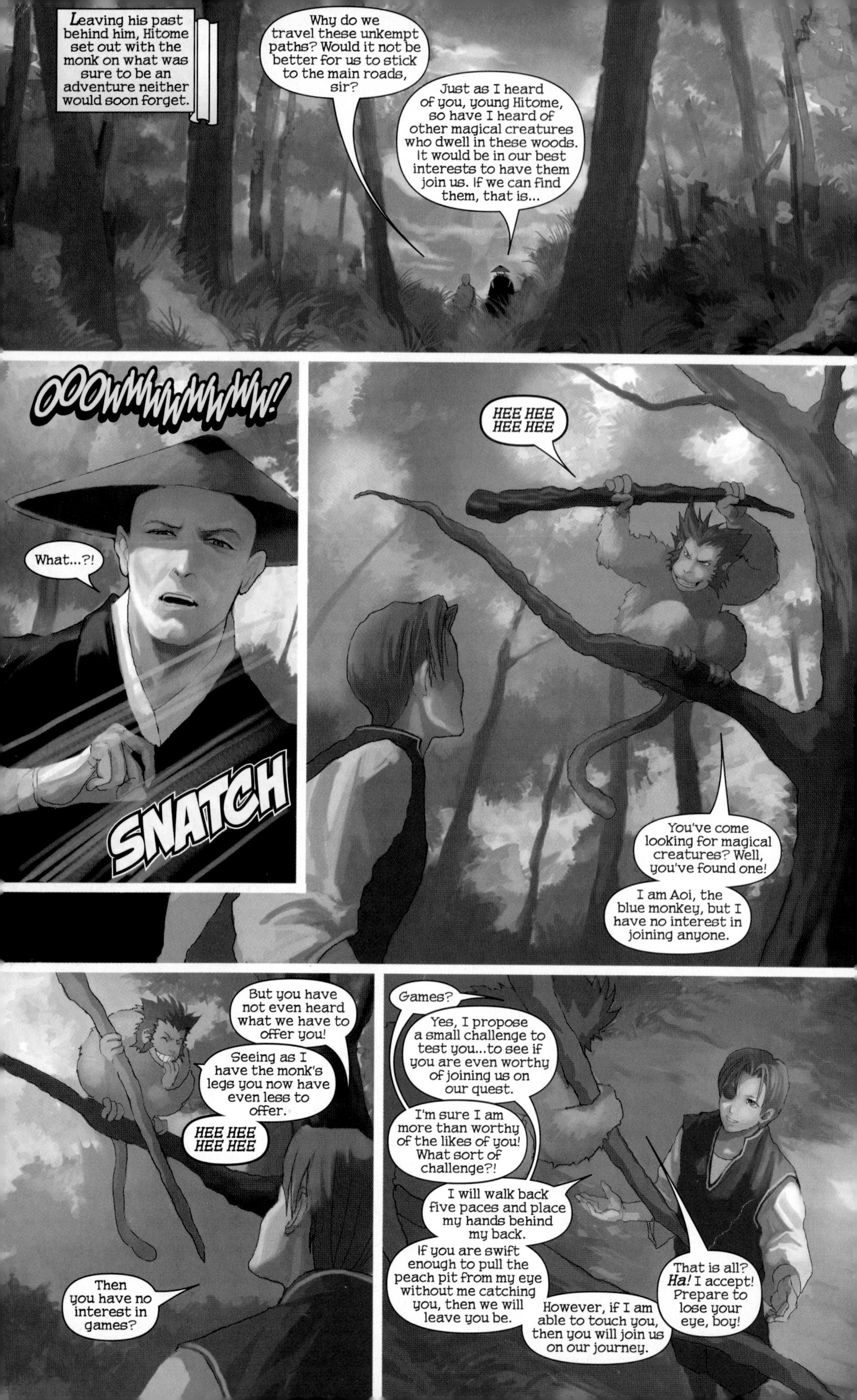
Leaving his past behind him, Hitome set out with the monk on what was sure to be an adventure neither would soon forget.
Why do we travel these unkempt paths? Would it not be better for us to stick to the main roads, sir?
Just as I heard of you, young Hitome, so have I heard of other magical creatures who dwell in these woods. It would be in our best interests to have them join us. If we can find them, that is...
OOOWWWWWWWWW!
What...?!
SNATCH
HEE HEE HEE HEE
You've come looking for magical creatures? Well, you've found one!
I am Aoi, the blue monkey, but I have no interest in joining anyone.
But you have not even heard what we have to offer you!
Seeing as I have the monk's legs you now have even less to offer.
HEE HEE HEE HEE
Then you have no interest in games?
Games?
Yes, I propose a small challenge to test you...to see if you are even worthy of joining us on our quest.
I'm sure I am more than worthy of the likes of you! What sort of challenge?!
I will walk back five paces and place my hands behind my back.
If you are swift enough to pull the peach pit from my eye without me catching you, then we will leave you be.
However, if I am able to touch you, then you will join us on our journey.
That is all? Ha! I accept! Prepare to lose your eye, boy!

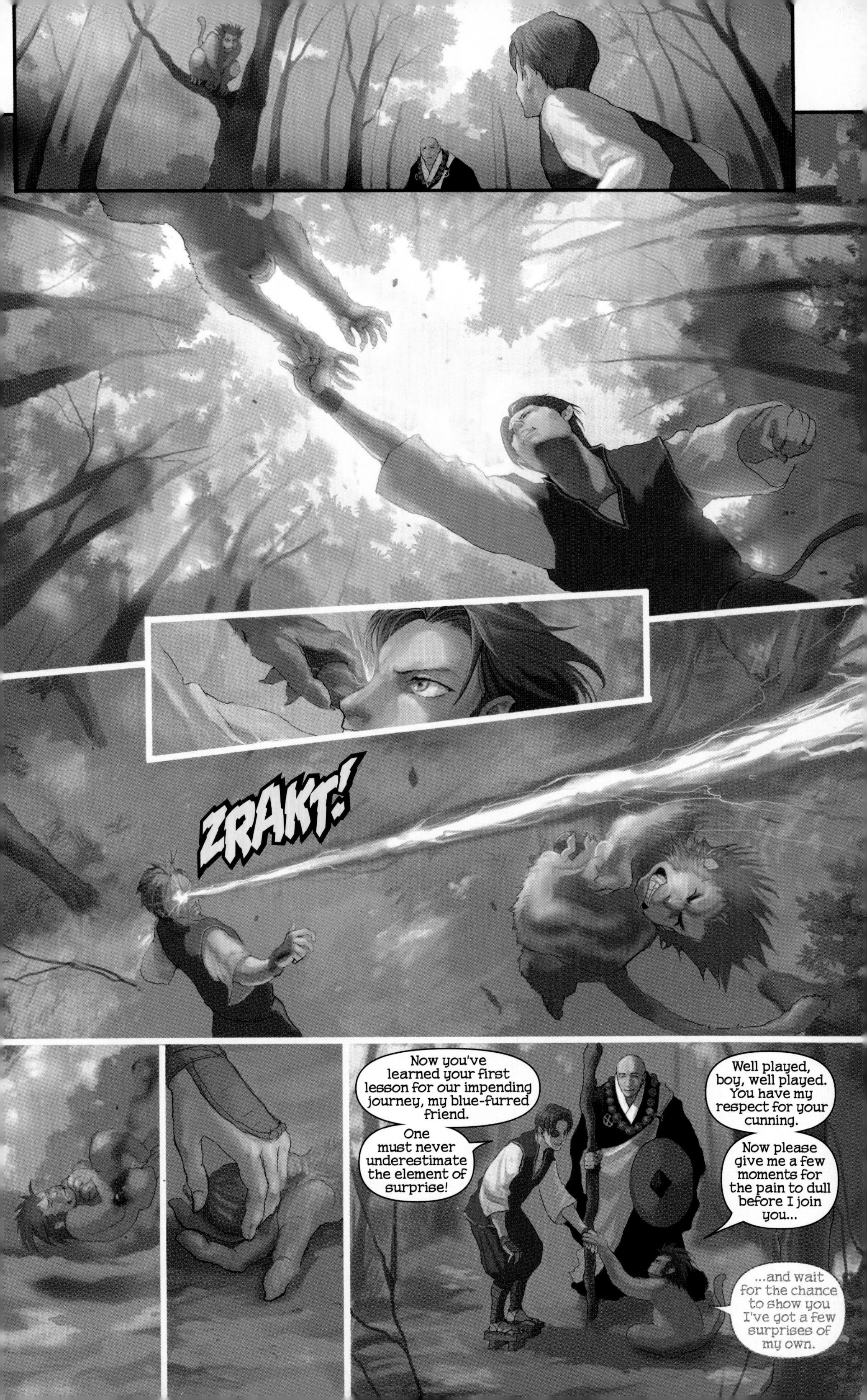
ZRAKT!
Now you've learned your first lesson for our impending journey, my blue-furred friend.
One must never underestimate the element of surprise!
Well played, boy, well played. You have my respect for your cunning.
Now please give me a few moments for the pain to dull before I join you...
...and wait for the chance to show you I've got a few surprises of my own.

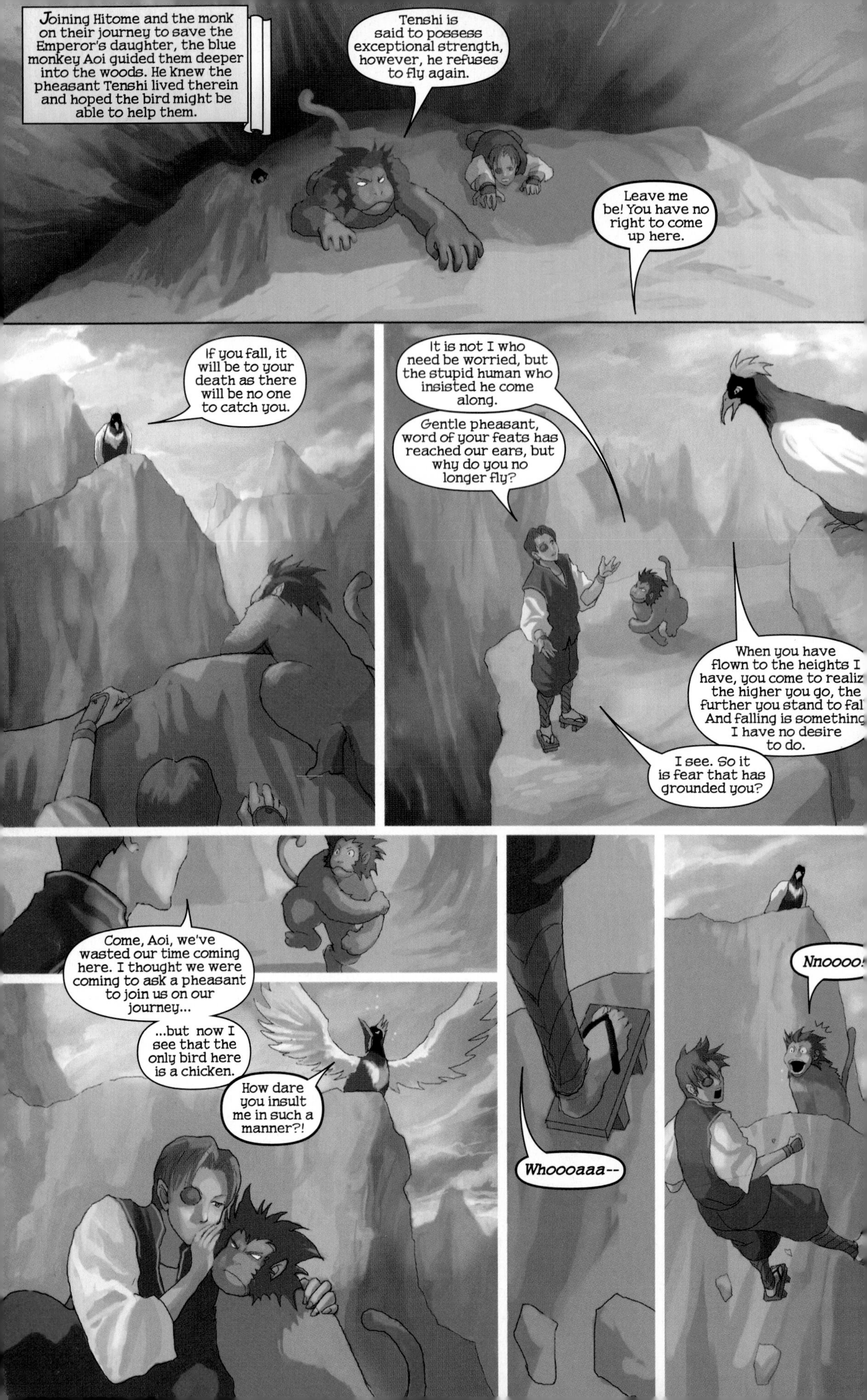

Joining Hitome and the monk on their journey to save the Emperor's daughter, the blue monkey Aoi guided them deeper into the woods. He knew the pheasant Tenshi lived therein and hoped the bird might be able to help them.
Tenshi is said to possess exceptional strength, however, he refuses to fly again.
Leave me be! You have no right to come up here.
If you fall, it will be to your death as there will be no one to catch you.
It is not I who need be worried, but the stupid human who insisted he come along.
Gentle pheasant, word of your feats has reached our ears, but why do you no longer fly?
When you have flown to the heights I have, you come to realiz the higher you go, the further you stand to fal And falling is somethin I have no desire to do.
I see. So it is fear that has grounded you?
Come, Aoi, we've wasted our time coming here. I thought we were coming to ask a pheasant to join us on our journey...
...but now I see that the only bird here is a chicken.
How dare you insult me in such a manner?!
Whoooaaa--
Nnoooo!

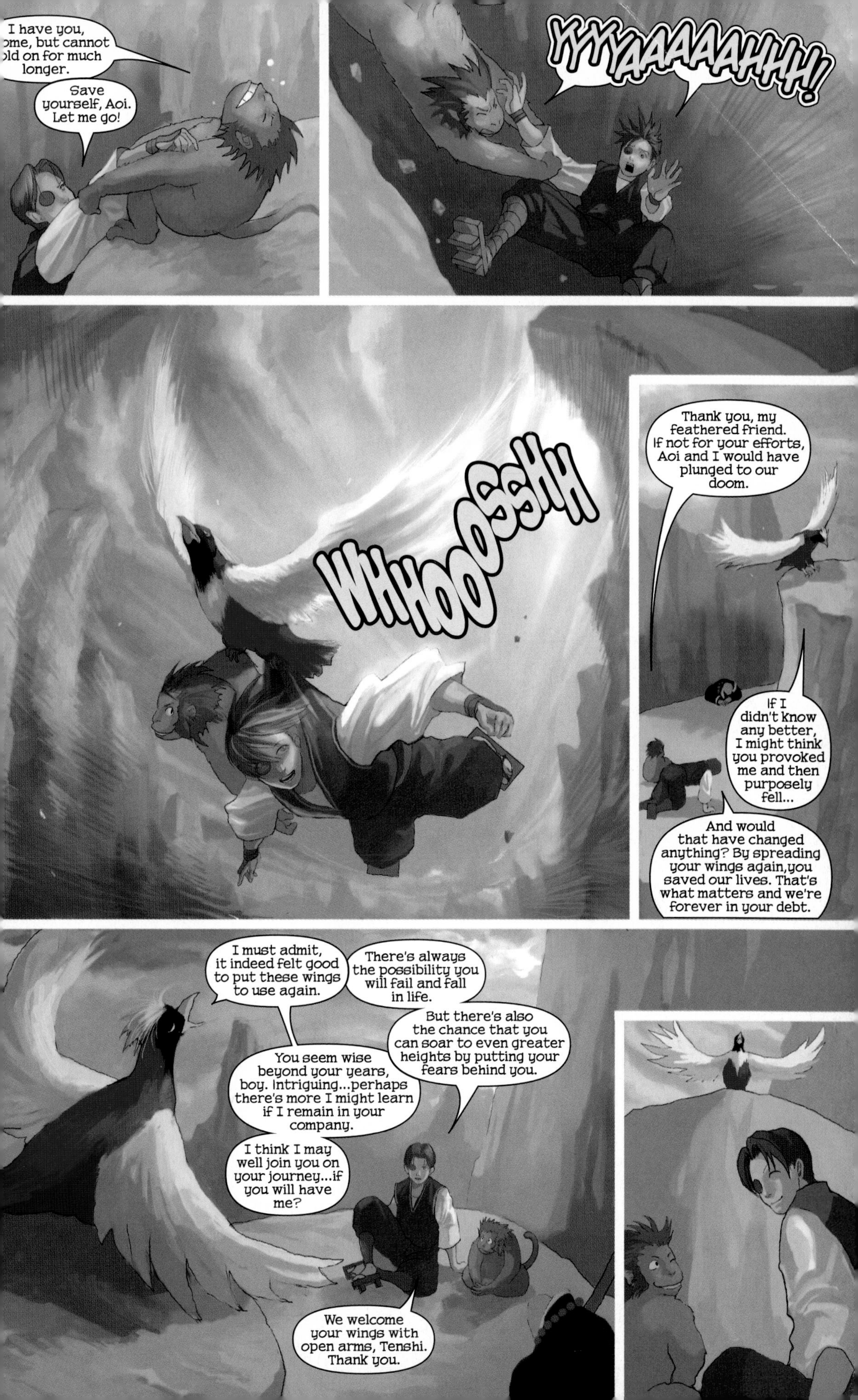

I have you, ...ome, but cannot ...old on for much longer.
Save yourself, Aoi. Let me go!
YYYAAAAAHHH!
WHHOOOSSHH
Thank you, my feathered friend. If not for your efforts, Aoi and I would have plunged to our doom.
If I didn't know any better, I might think you provoked me and then purposely fell...
And would that have changed anything? By spreading your wings again, you saved our lives. That's what matters and we're forever in your debt.
I must admit, it indeed felt good to put these wings to use again.
There's always the possibility you will fail and fall in life.
But there's also the chance that you can soar to even greater heights by putting your fears behind you.
You seem wise beyond your years, boy. Intriguing...perhaps there's more I might learn if I remain in your company.
I think I may well join you on your journey...if you will have me?
We welcome your wings with open arms, Tenshi. Thank you.

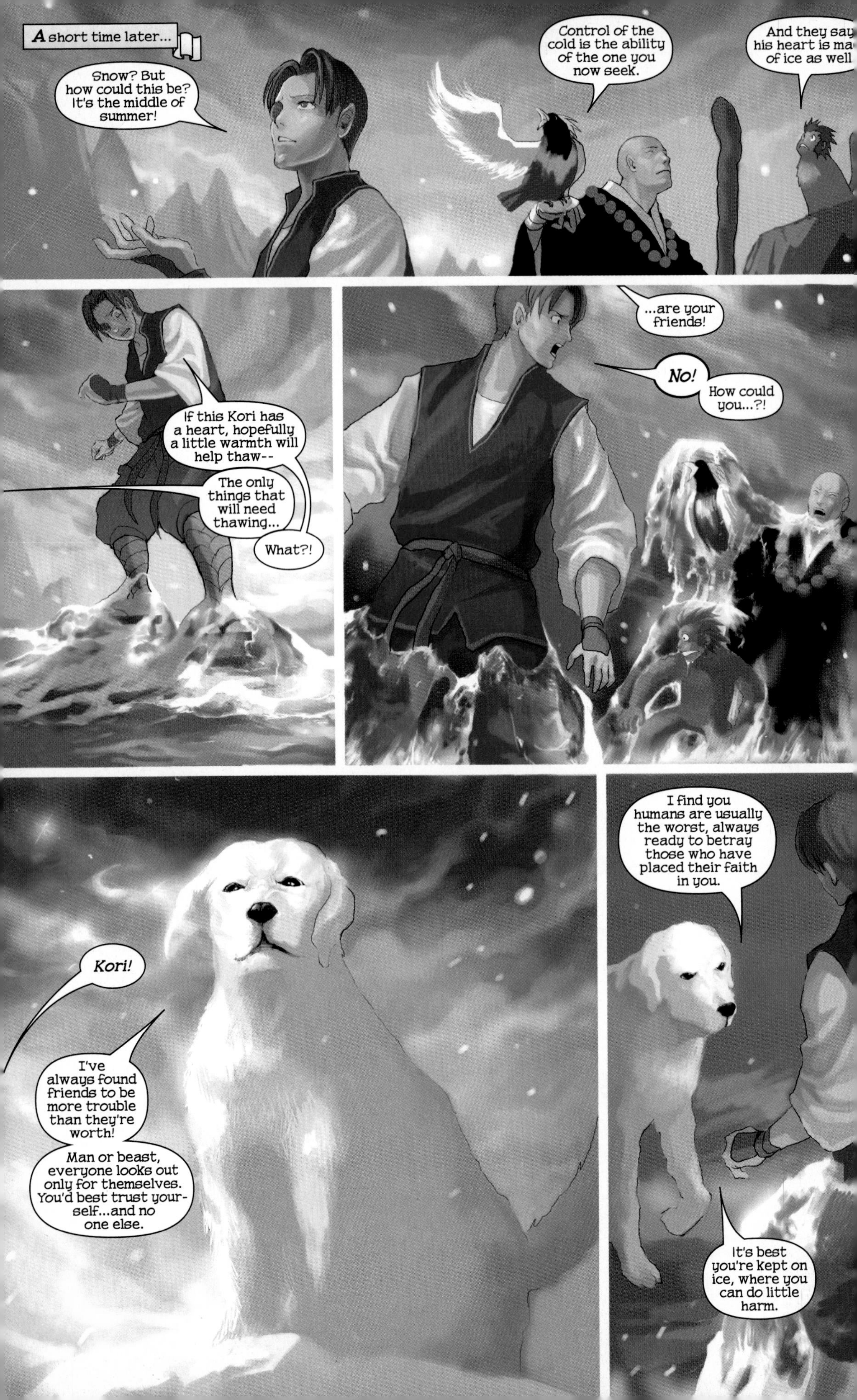
A short time later...
Snow? But how could this be? It's the middle of summer!
Control of the cold is the ability of the one you now seek.
And they say his heart is ma of ice as well
If this Kori has a heart, hopefully a little warmth will help thaw--
The only things that will need thawing...
What?!
...are your friends!
No!
How could you...?!
Kori!
I've always found friends to be more trouble than they're worth!
Man or beast, everyone looks out only for themselves. You'd best trust your-self...and no one else.
I find you humans are usually the worst, always ready to betray those who have placed their faith in you.
It's best you're kept on ice, where you can do little harm.

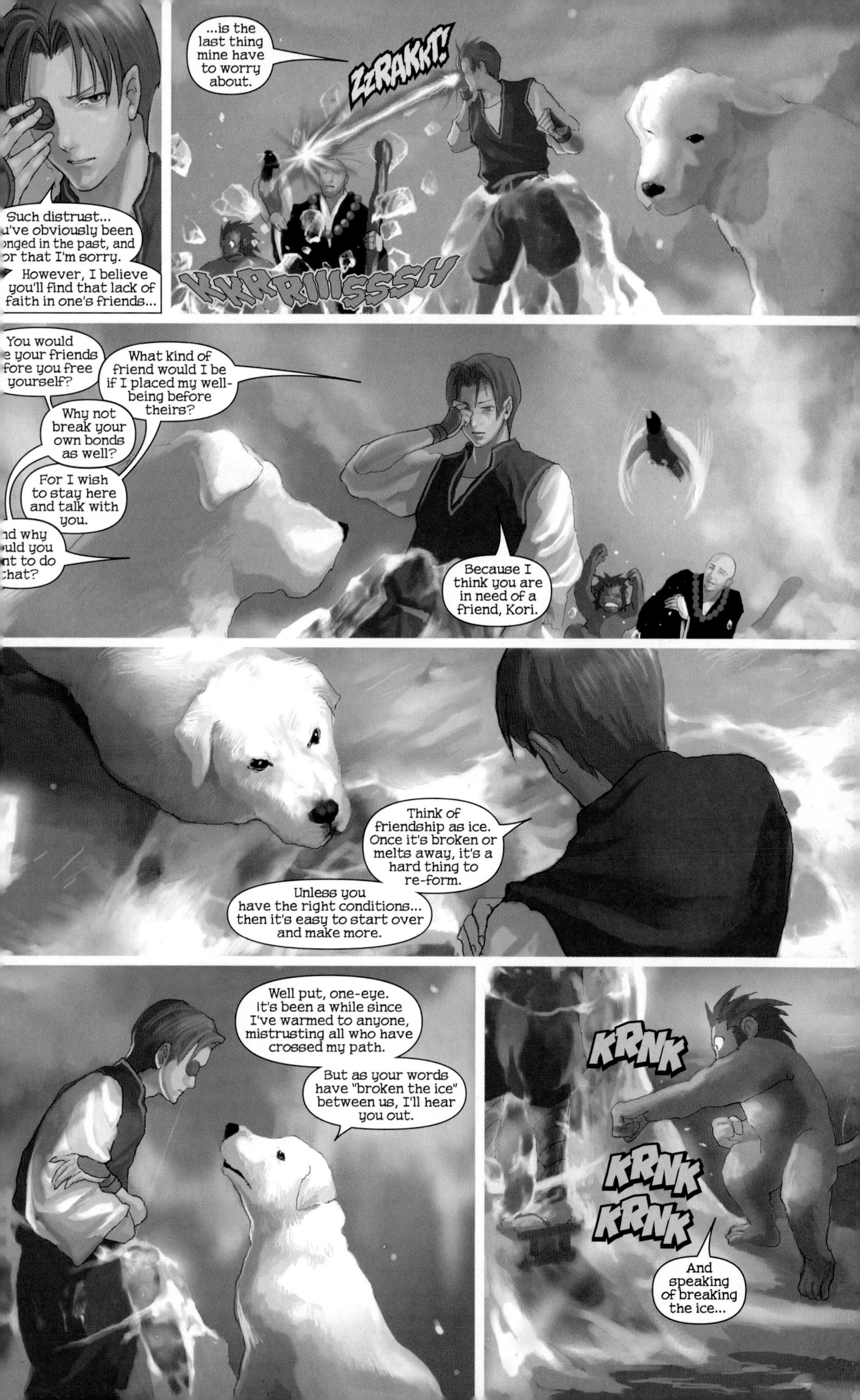

Such distrust...
u've obviously been
onged in the past, and
or that I'm sorry.
However, I believe you'll find that lack of faith in one's friends...
...is the last thing mine have to worry about.
ZzRAKKT!
KKRRIIISSSSH
You would
e your friends
fore you free
yourself?
What kind of friend would I be if I placed my well-being before theirs?
Why not break your own bonds as well?
For I wish to stay here and talk with you.
nd why
uld you
nt to do
that?
Because I think you are in need of a friend, Kori.
Think of friendship as ice. Once it's broken or melts away, it's a hard thing to re-form.
Unless you have the right conditions... then it's easy to start over and make more.
Well put, one-eye. It's been a while since I've warmed to anyone, mistrusting all who have crossed my path.
But as your words have "broken the ice" between us, I'll hear you out.
KRNK
KRNK
KRNK
And speaking of breaking the ice...

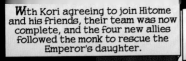

With Kori agreeing to join Hitome and his friends, their team was now complete, and the four new allies followed the monk to rescue the Emperor's daughter.

Something much easier said than done, though. Especially where demons are concerned!

The evil in the air here sends a chill up my spine.

Yes, we are approaching the demons' lair.

Let's stand tall and hope these creatures prove more myth than magic.

I hate to disappoint, bu I believe you w find we are fa from fiction a a force to b feared.

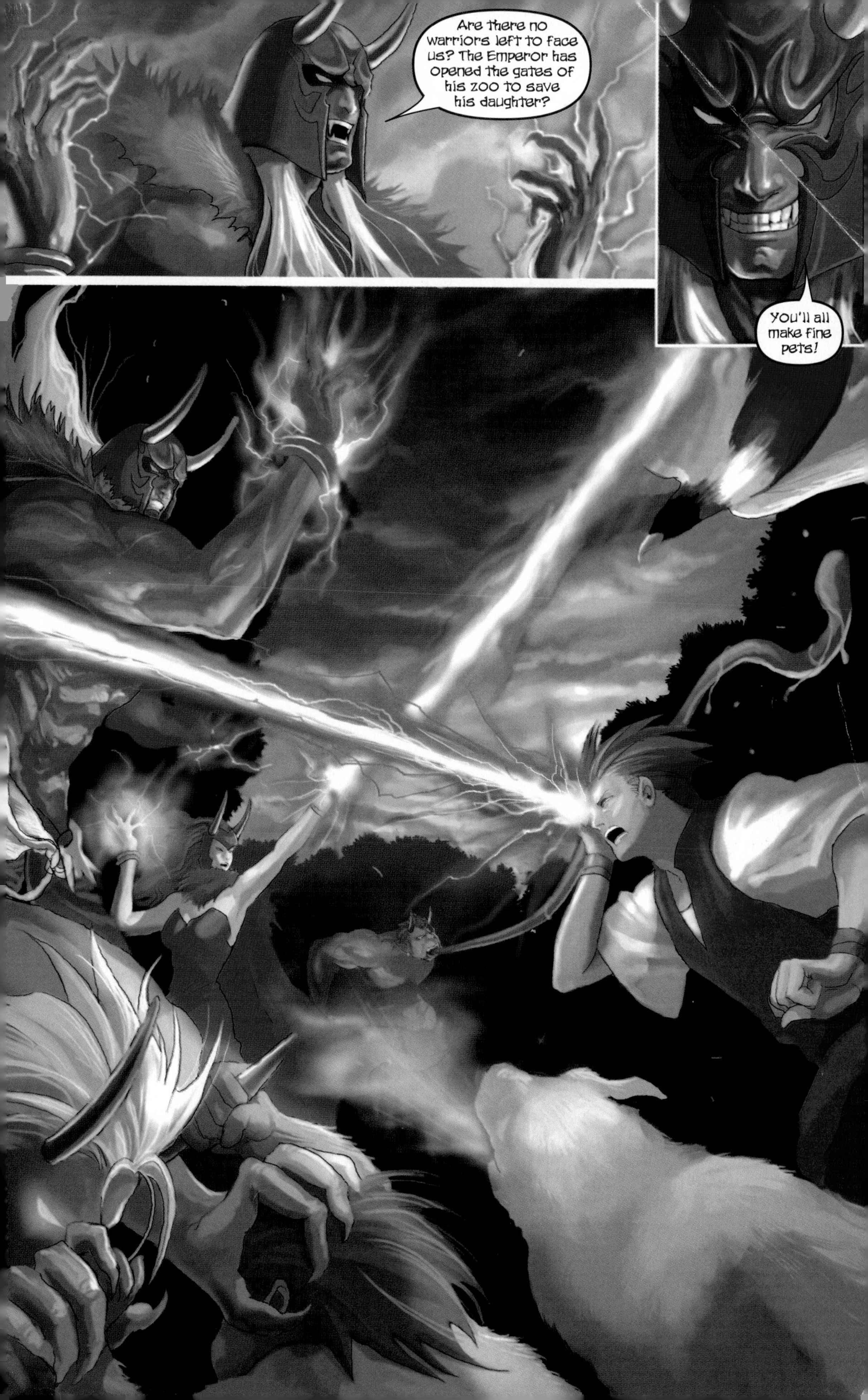
Are there no warriors left to face us? The Emperor has opened the gates of his zoo to save his daughter?
You'll all make fine pets!

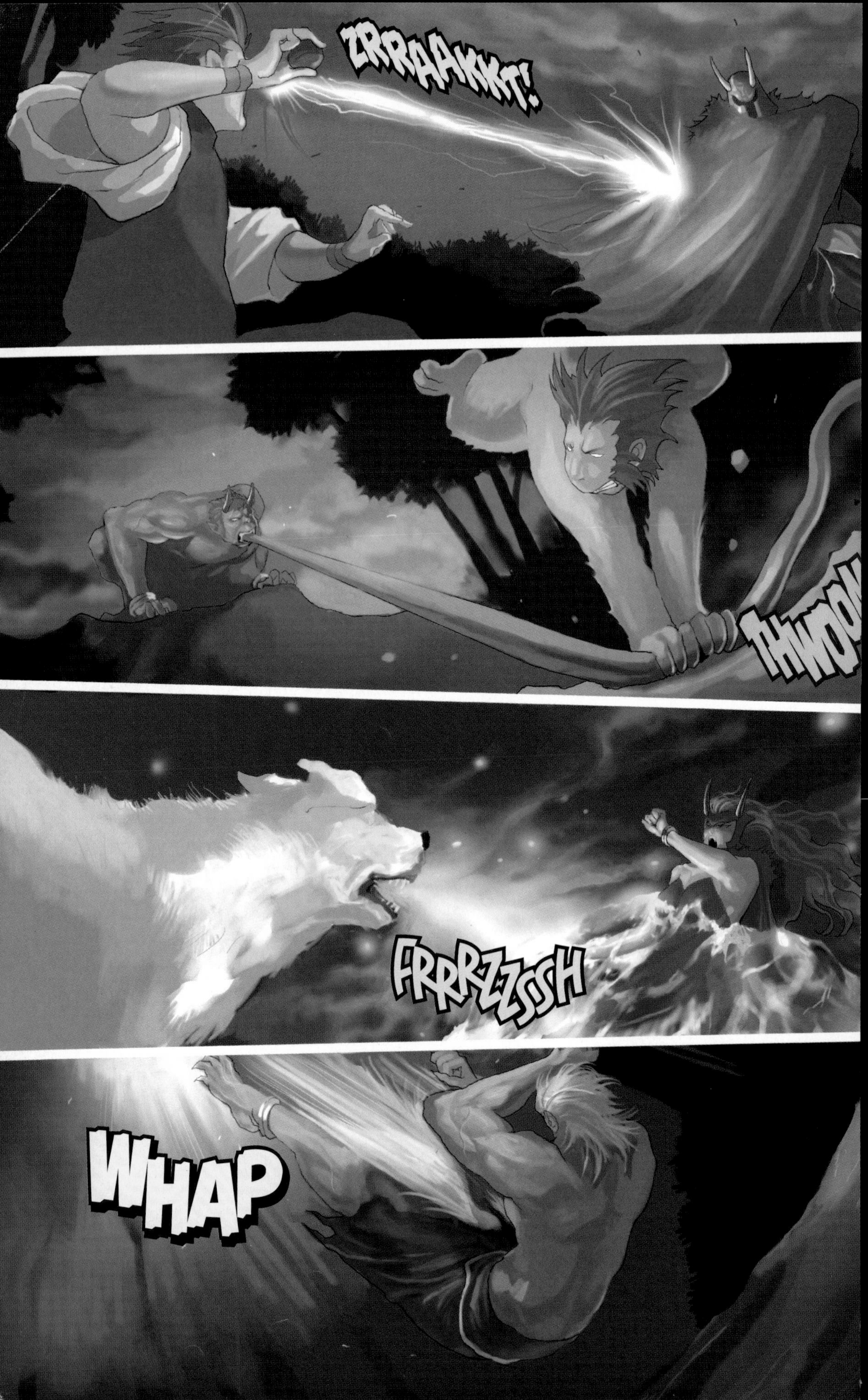
ZRRAAKKKT!
THWOOK
FRRRZZSSH
WHAP

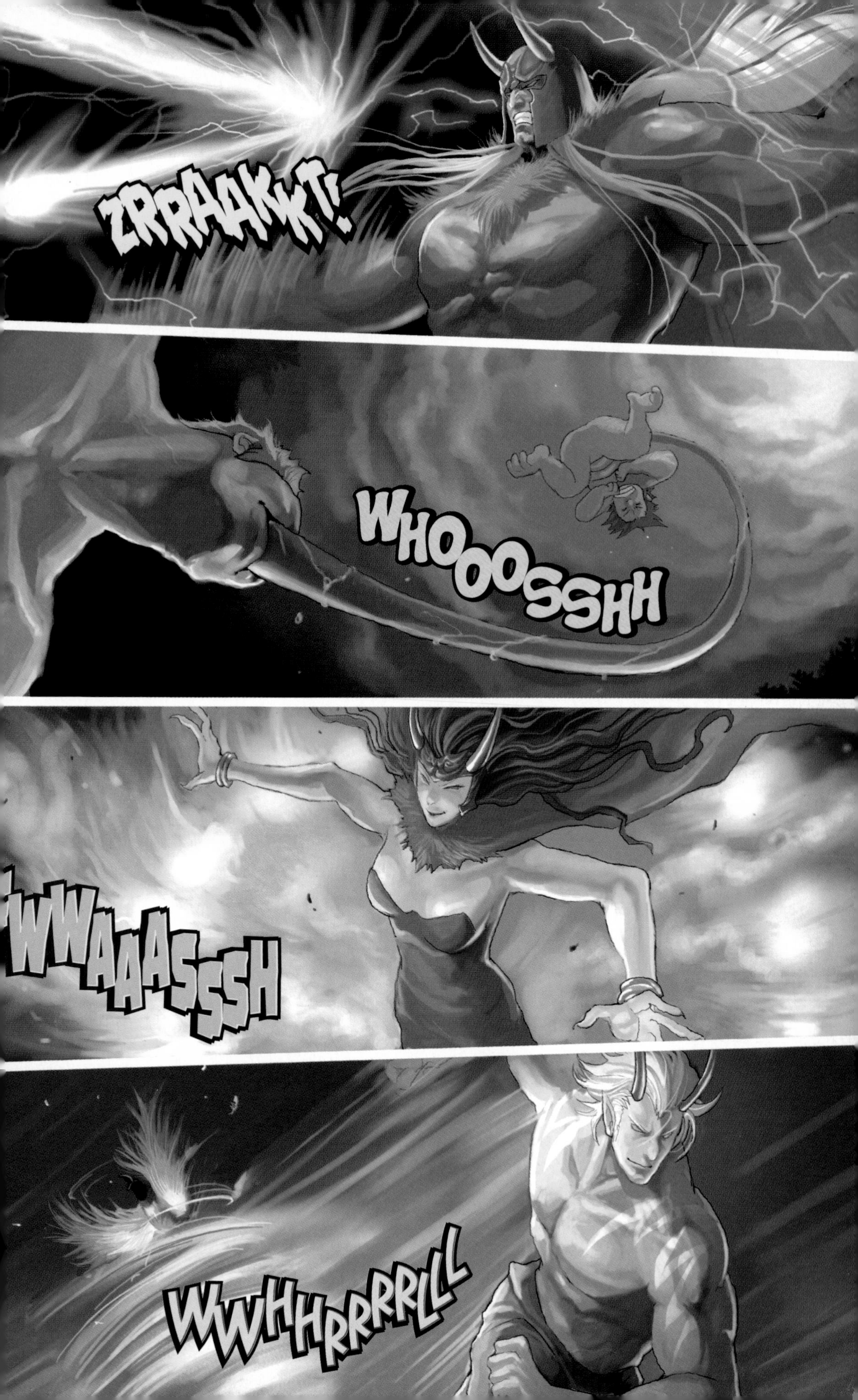
ZRRAAKKT!
WHOOOOSSHH
WWAAASSSH
WWHHRRRRLLL

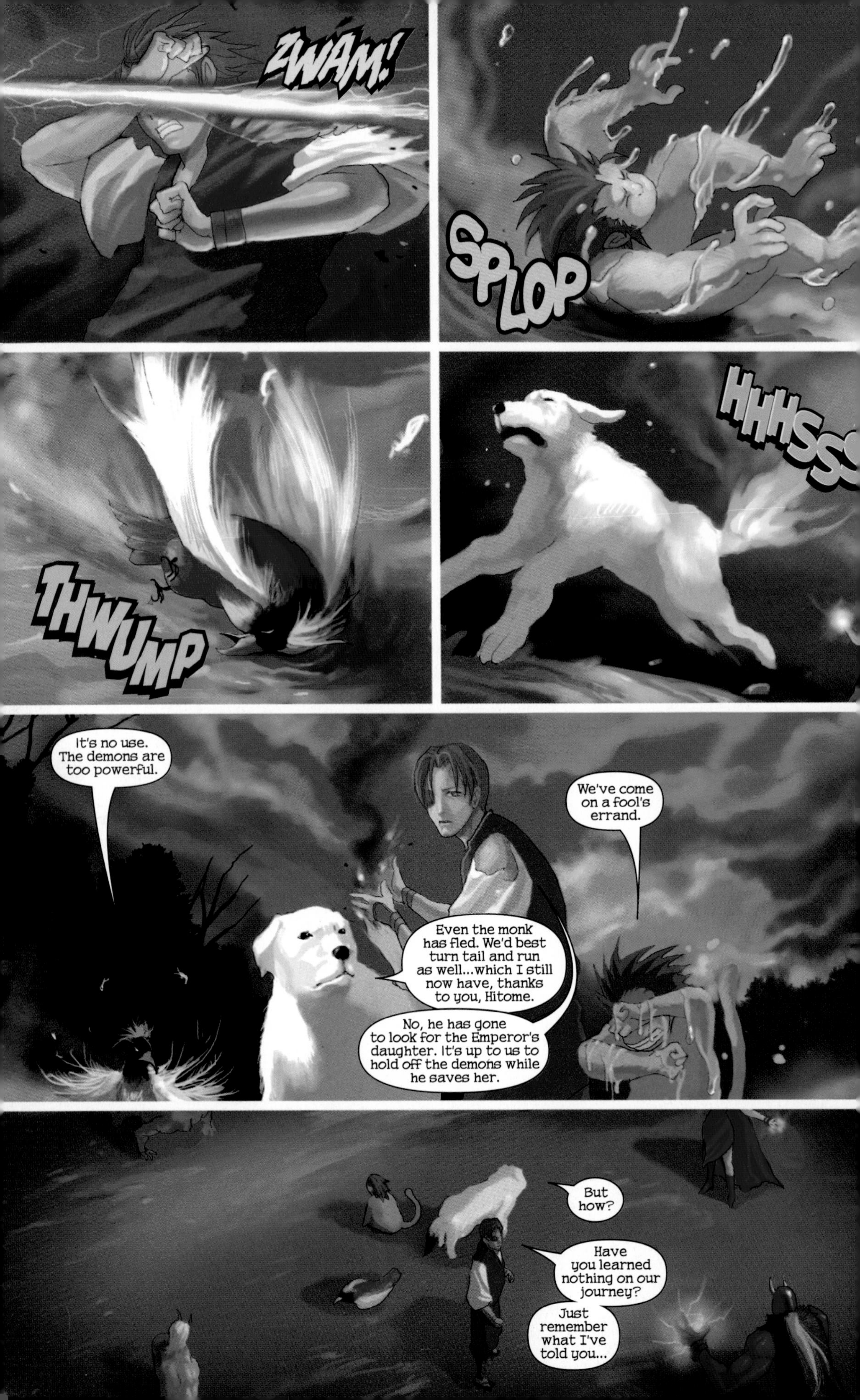
ZWAM!
SPLOP
THWUMP
HHHSSS
It's no use. The demons are too powerful.
We've come on a fool's errand.
Even the monk has fled. We'd best turn tail and run as well...which I still now have, thanks to you, Hitome.
No, he has gone to look for the Emperor's daughter. It's up to us to hold off the demons while he saves her.
But how?
Have you learned nothing on our journey?
Just remember what I've told you...

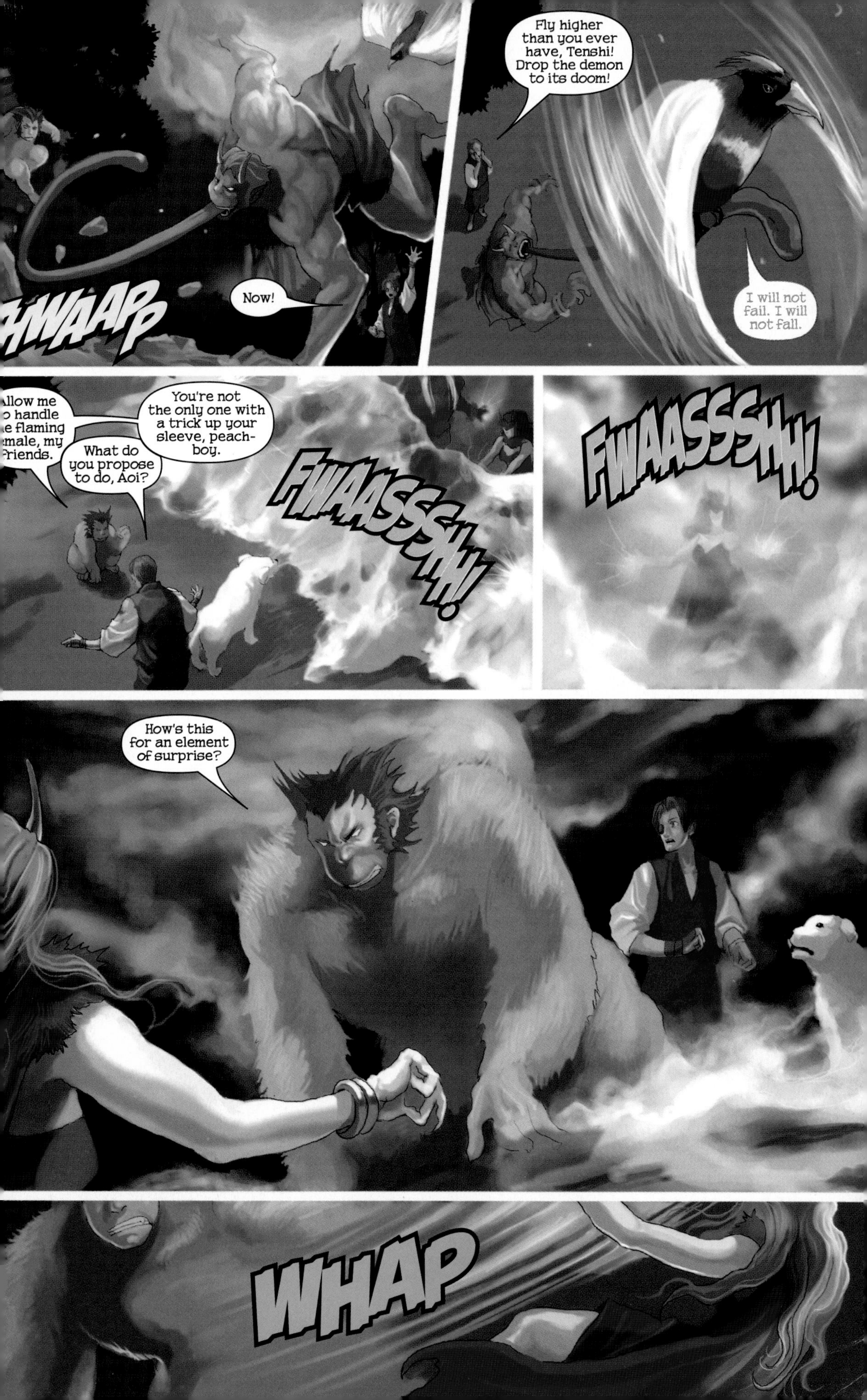

FWAAPP
Now!
Fly higher than you ever have, Tenshi! Drop the demon to its doom!
I will not fail. I will not fall.
Allow me to handle the flaming female, my friends.
You're not the only one with a trick up your sleeve, peach-boy.
What do you propose to do, Aoi?
FWAASSSHH!
FWAASSSHH!
How's this for an element of surprise?
WHAP

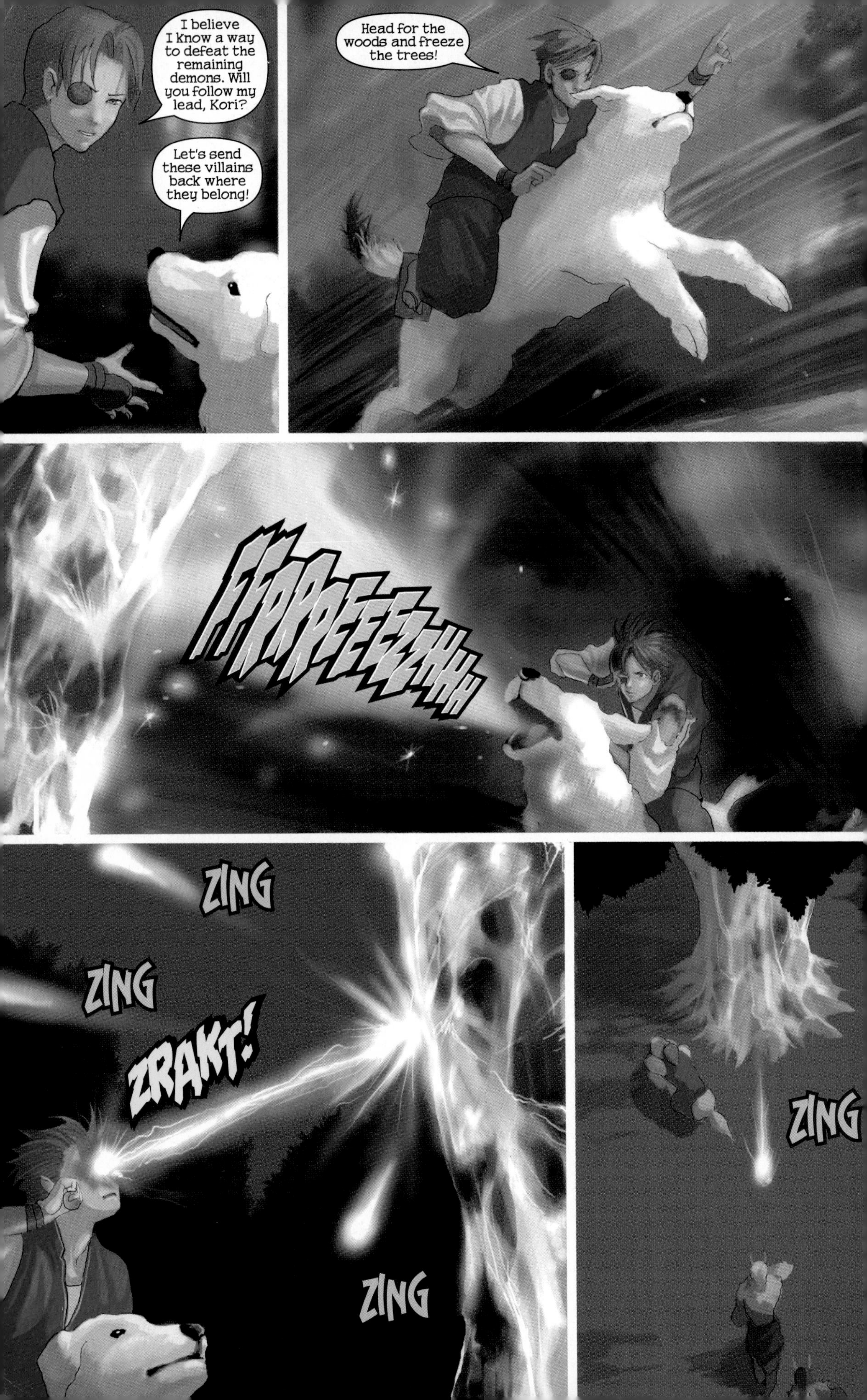
I believe I know a way to defeat the remaining demons. Will you follow my lead, Kori?
Let's send these villains back where they belong!
Head for the woods and freeze the trees!
FFFRREEEEZHHH
ZING
ZING
ZRAKT!
ZING
ZING

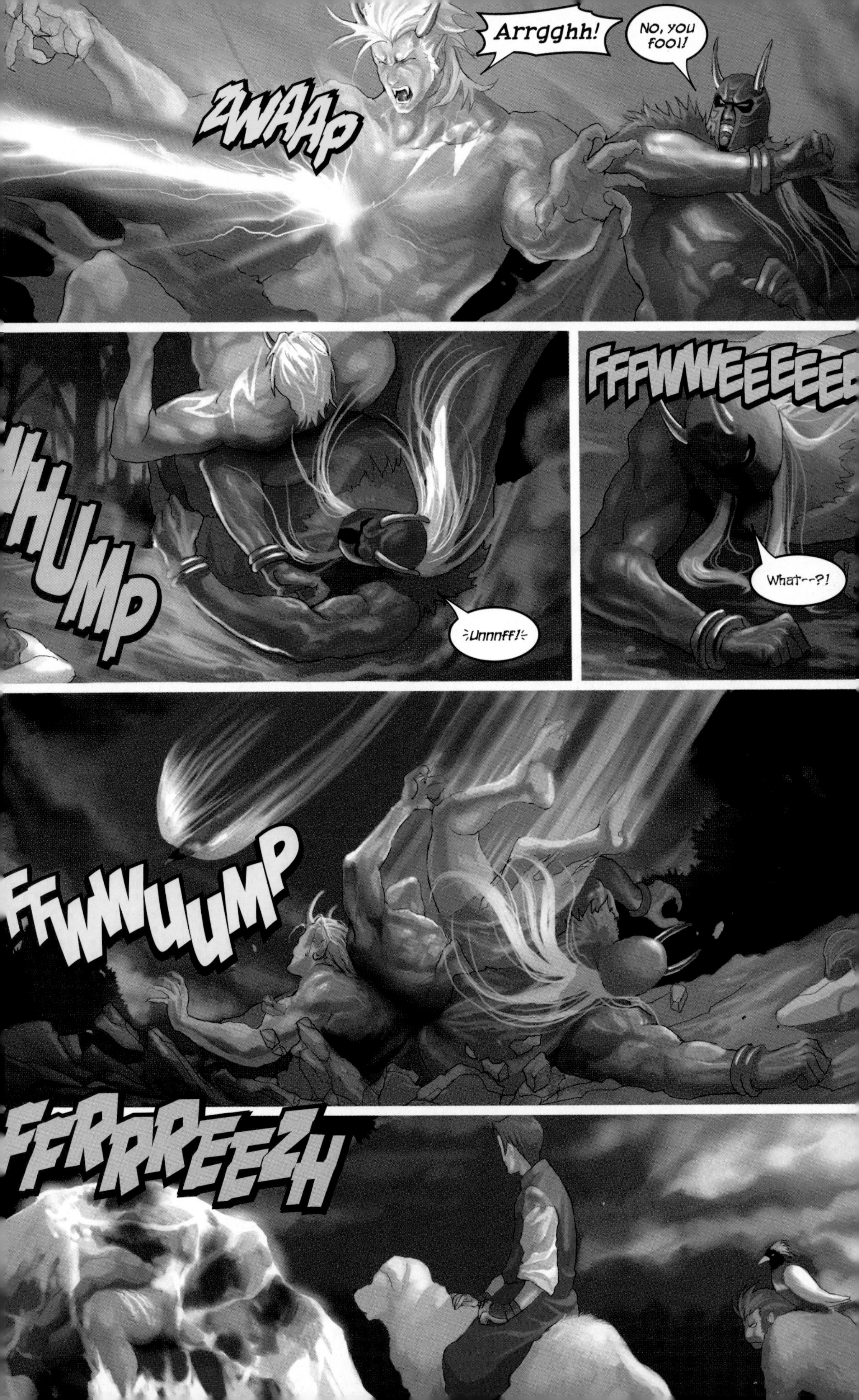

Arrgghh!
No, you fool!
ZWAAP
HUMP
Unnnff!
FFFWWEEEEEE
What--?!
FFWNUUMP
FFRRREEZH

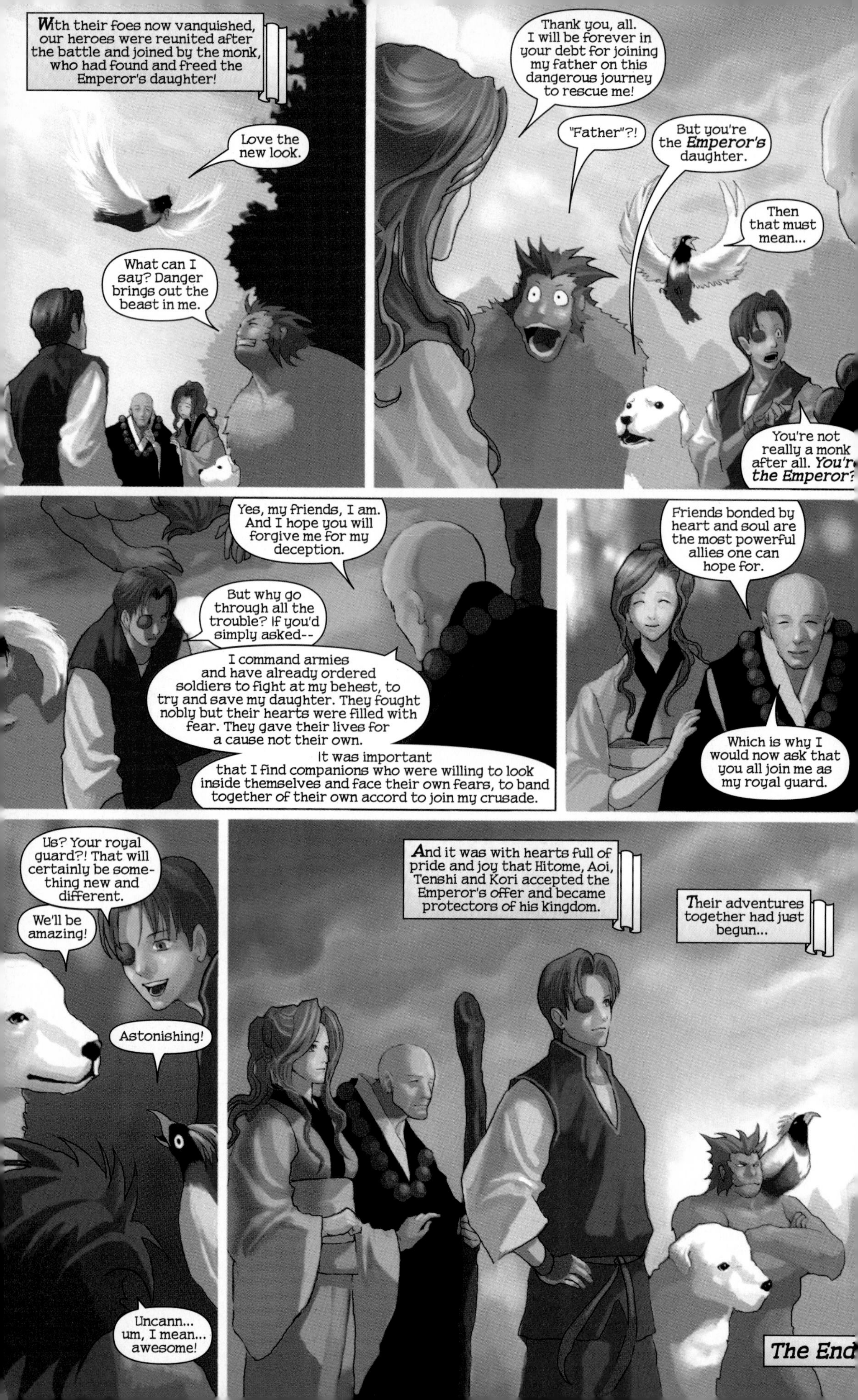
With their foes now vanquished, our heroes were reunited after the battle and joined by the monk, who had found and freed the Emperor's daughter!
Love the new look.
What can I say? Danger brings out the beast in me.
Thank you, all. I will be forever in your debt for joining my father on this dangerous journey to rescue me!
"Father"?!
But you're the Emperor's daughter.
Then that must mean...
You're not really a monk after all. You'r the Emperor?
Yes, my friends, I am. And I hope you will forgive me for my deception.
But why go through all the trouble? If you'd simply asked--
I command armies and have already ordered soldiers to fight at my behest, to try and save my daughter. They fought nobly but their hearts were filled with fear. They gave their lives for a cause not their own.
It was important that I find companions who were willing to look inside themselves and face their own fears, to band together of their own accord to join my crusade.
Friends bonded by heart and soul are the most powerful allies one can hope for.
Which is why I would now ask that you all join me as my royal guard.
Us? Your royal guard?! That will certainly be some-thing new and different.
We'll be amazing!
Astonishing!
Uncann... um, I mean... awesome!
And it was with hearts full of pride and joy that Hitome, Aoi, Tenshi and Kori accepted the Emperor's offer and became protectors of his kingdom.
Their adventures together had just begun...
The End

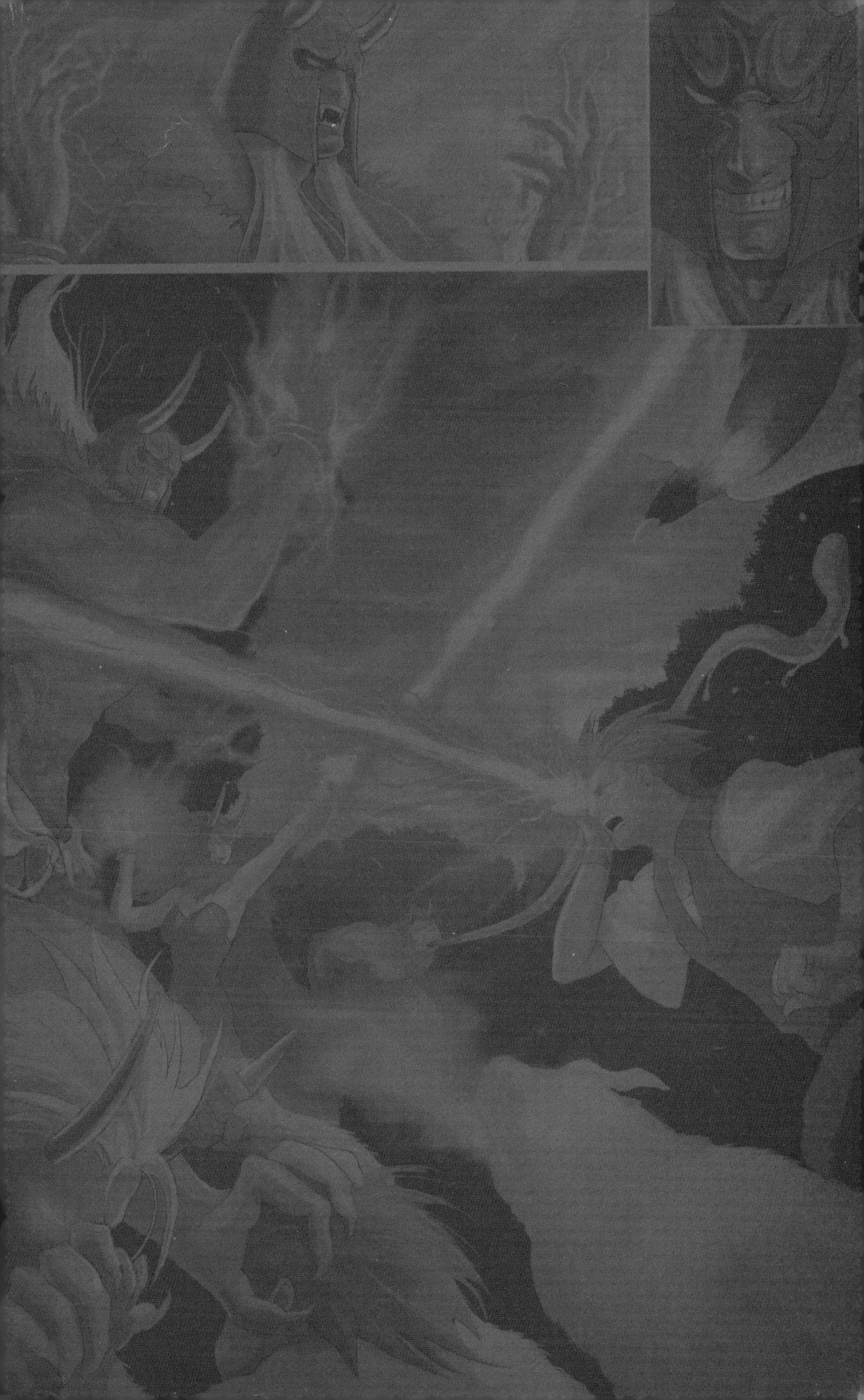

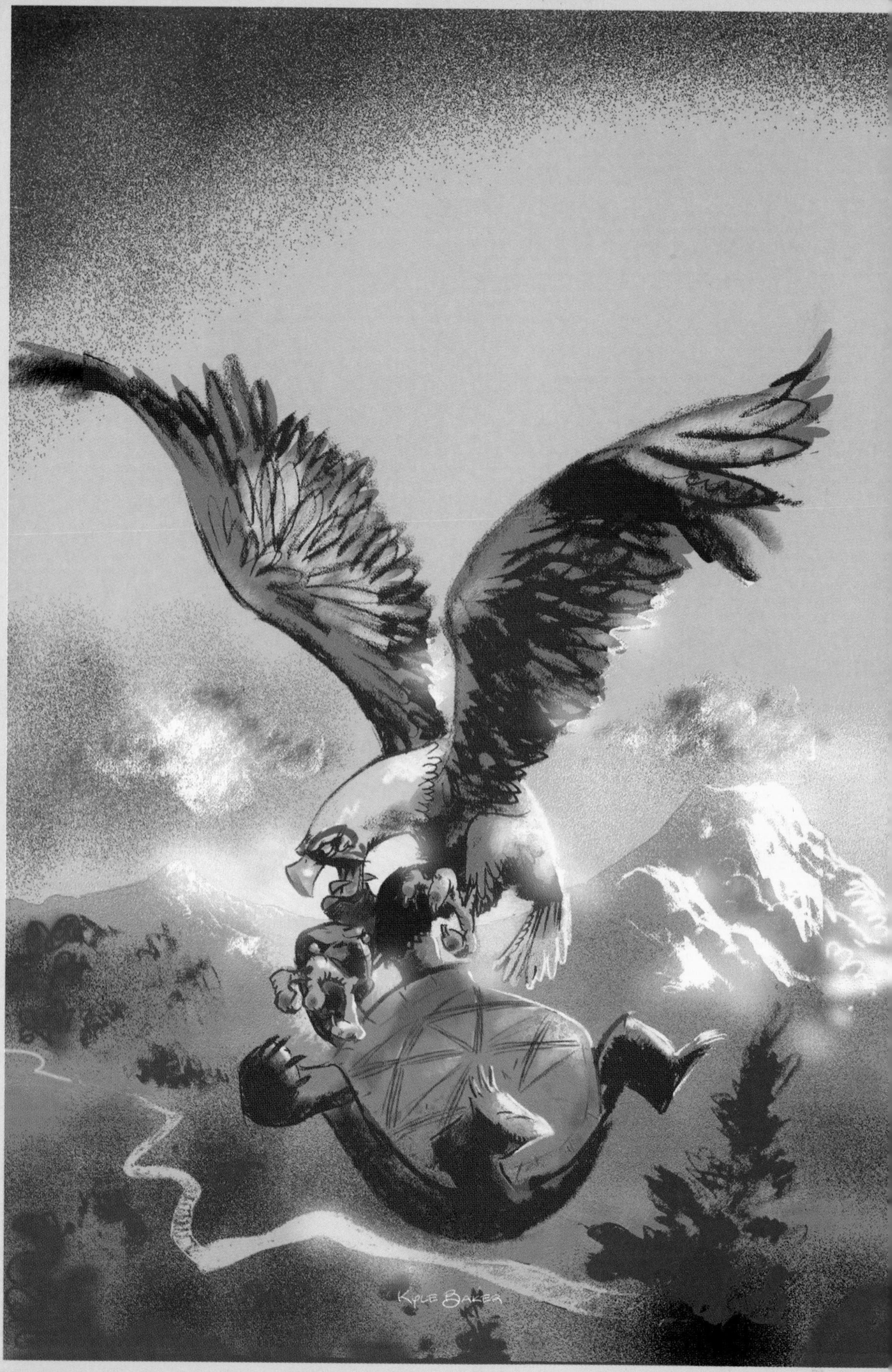
KYLE BAKER

FAITH IN FRIENDS

Inspired by the African fairy tale, *"The Friendship of the Tortoise and the Eagle"*

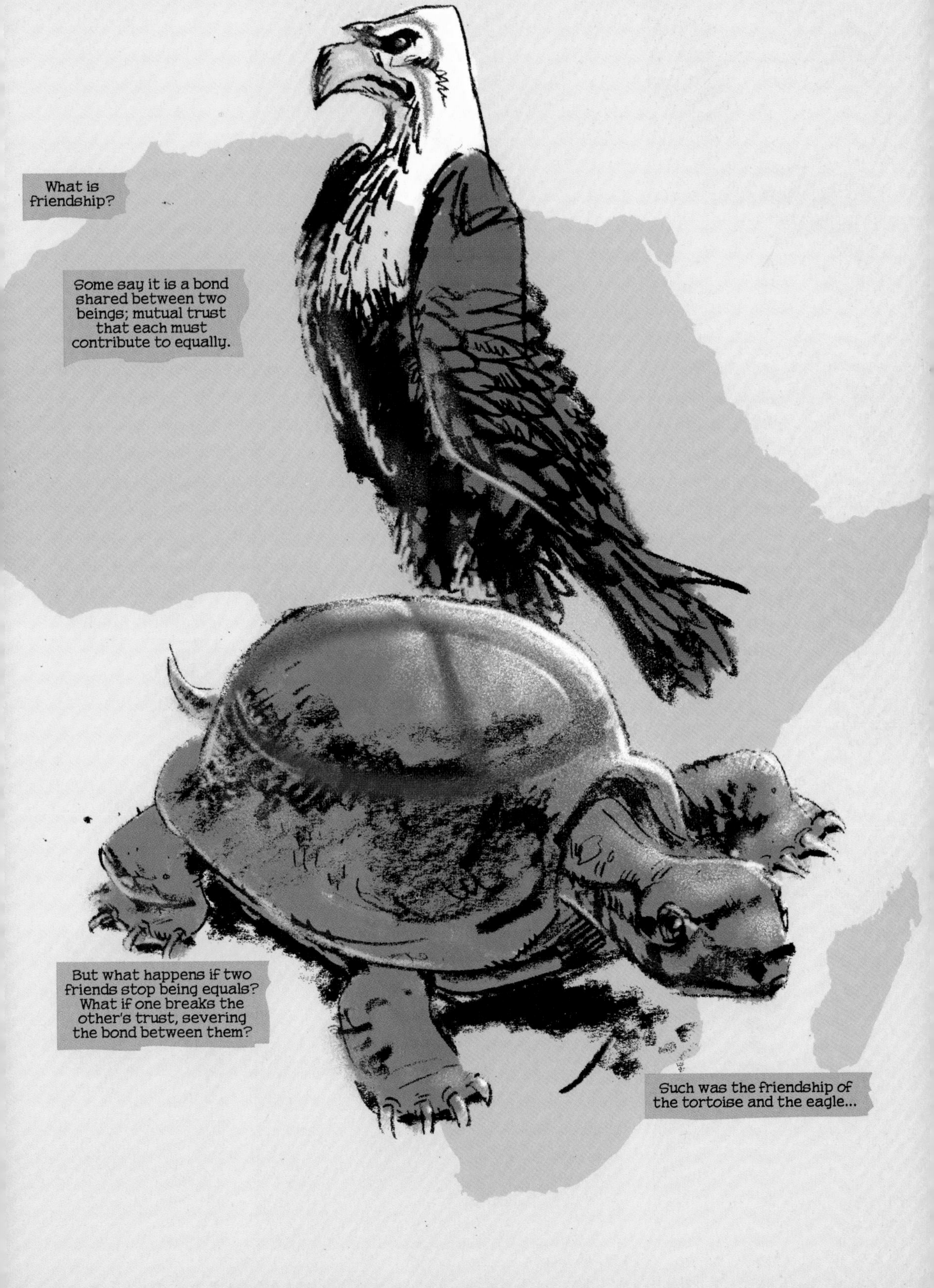
What is friendship?
Some say it is a bond shared between two beings; mutual trust that each must contribute to equally.
But what happens if two friends stop being equals? What if one breaks the other's trust, severing the bond between them?
Such was the friendship of the tortoise and the eagle...

Their upbringing could not have been more different.

The eagle chick witnessed his family's slaughter.

He learned the brutal reality hatred.

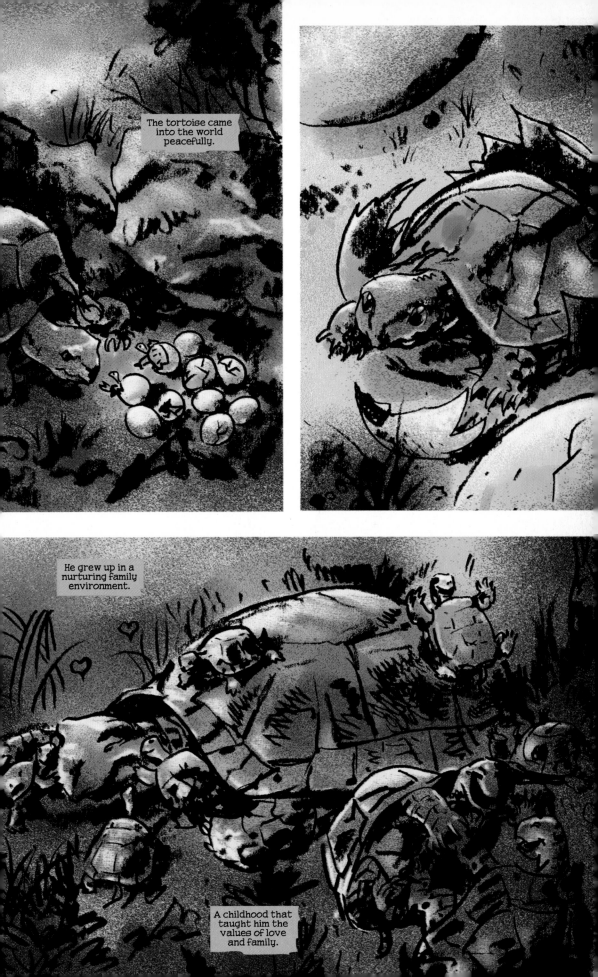

The tortoise came into the world peacefully.

He grew up in a nurturing family environment.

A childhood that taught him the values of love and family.

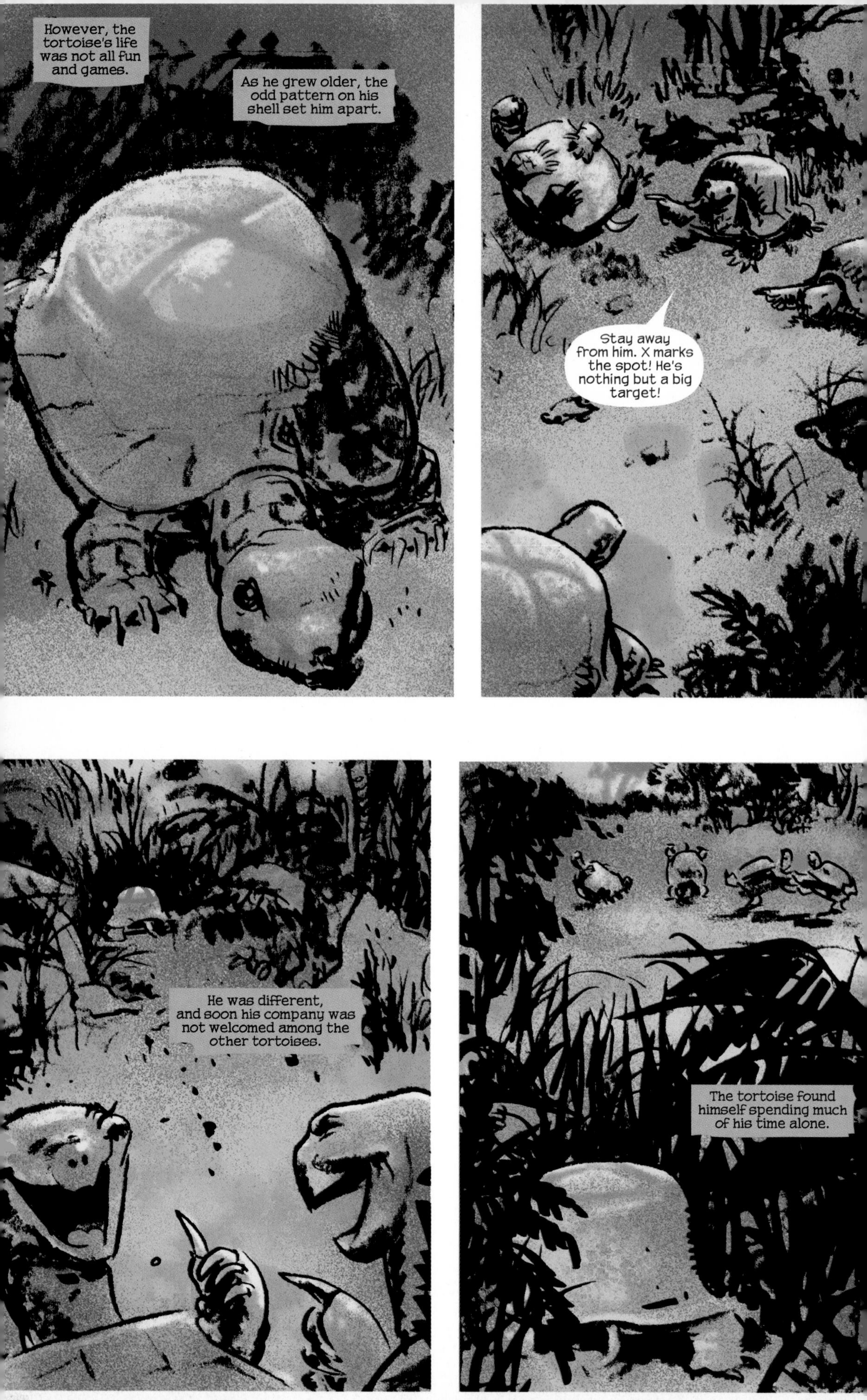
However, the tortoise's life was not all fun and games.
As he grew older, the odd pattern on his shell set him apart.
Stay away from him. X marks the spot! He's nothing but a big target!
He was different, and soon his company was not welcomed among the other tortoises.
The tortoise found himself spending much of his time alone.

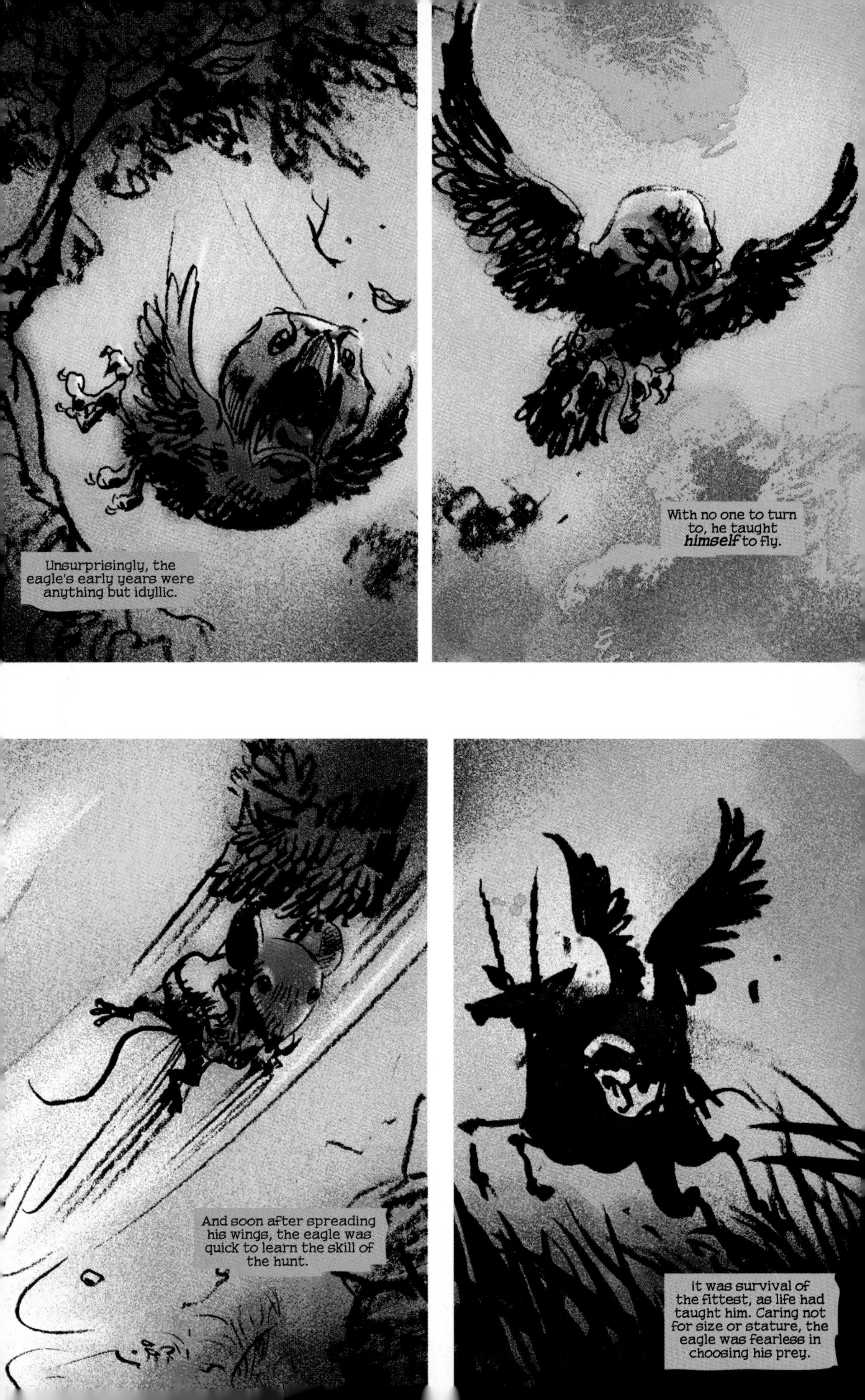
Unsurprisingly, the eagle's early years were anything but idyllic.
With no one to turn to, he taught *himself* to fly.
And soon after spreading his wings, the eagle was quick to learn the skill of the hunt.
It was survival of the fittest, as life had taught him. Caring not for size or stature, the eagle was fearless in choosing his prey.

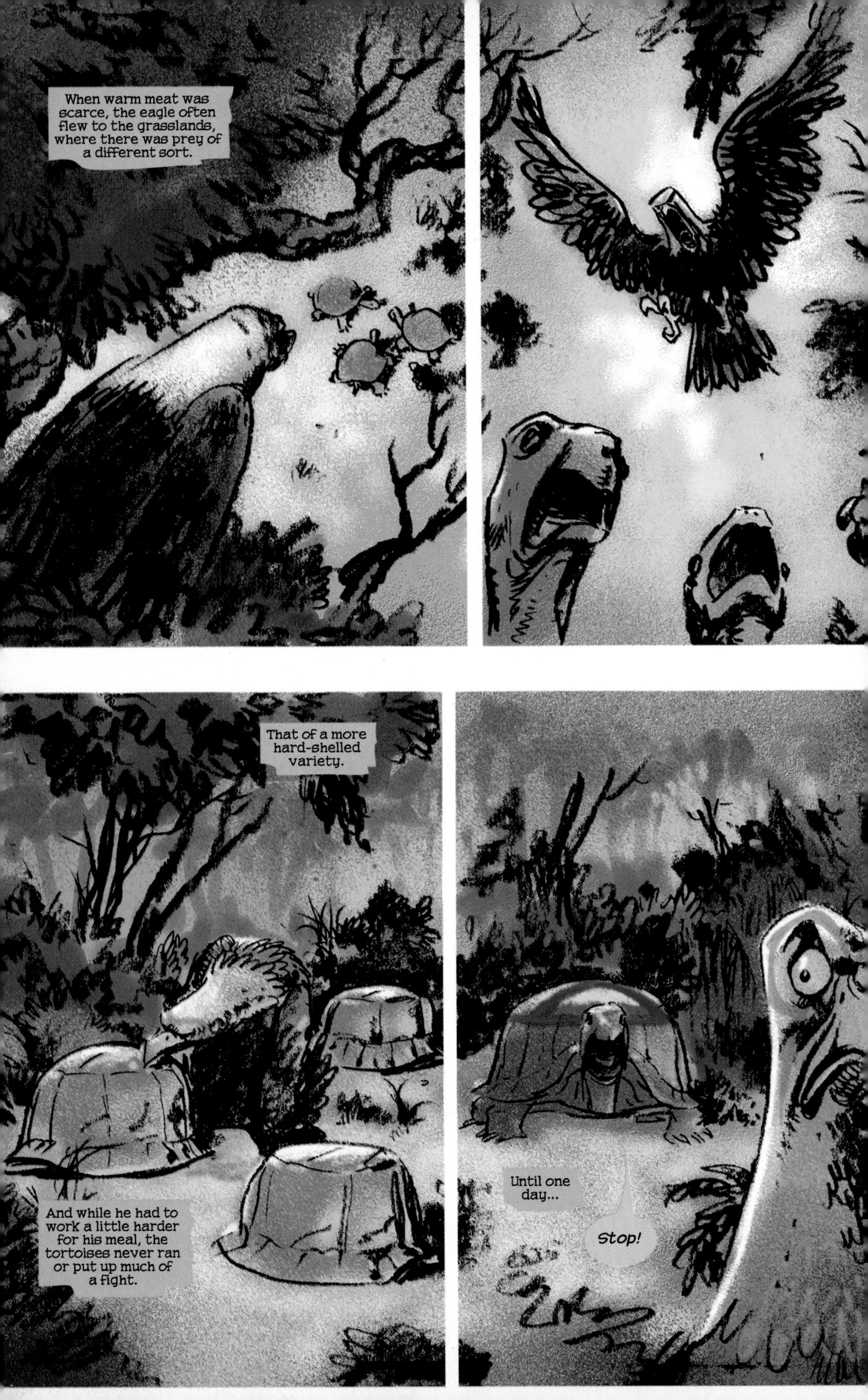
When warm meat was scarce, the eagle often flew to the grasslands, where there was prey of a different sort.
That of a more hard-shelled variety.
And while he had to work a little harder for his meal, the tortoises never ran or put up much of a fight.
Until one day...
Stop!

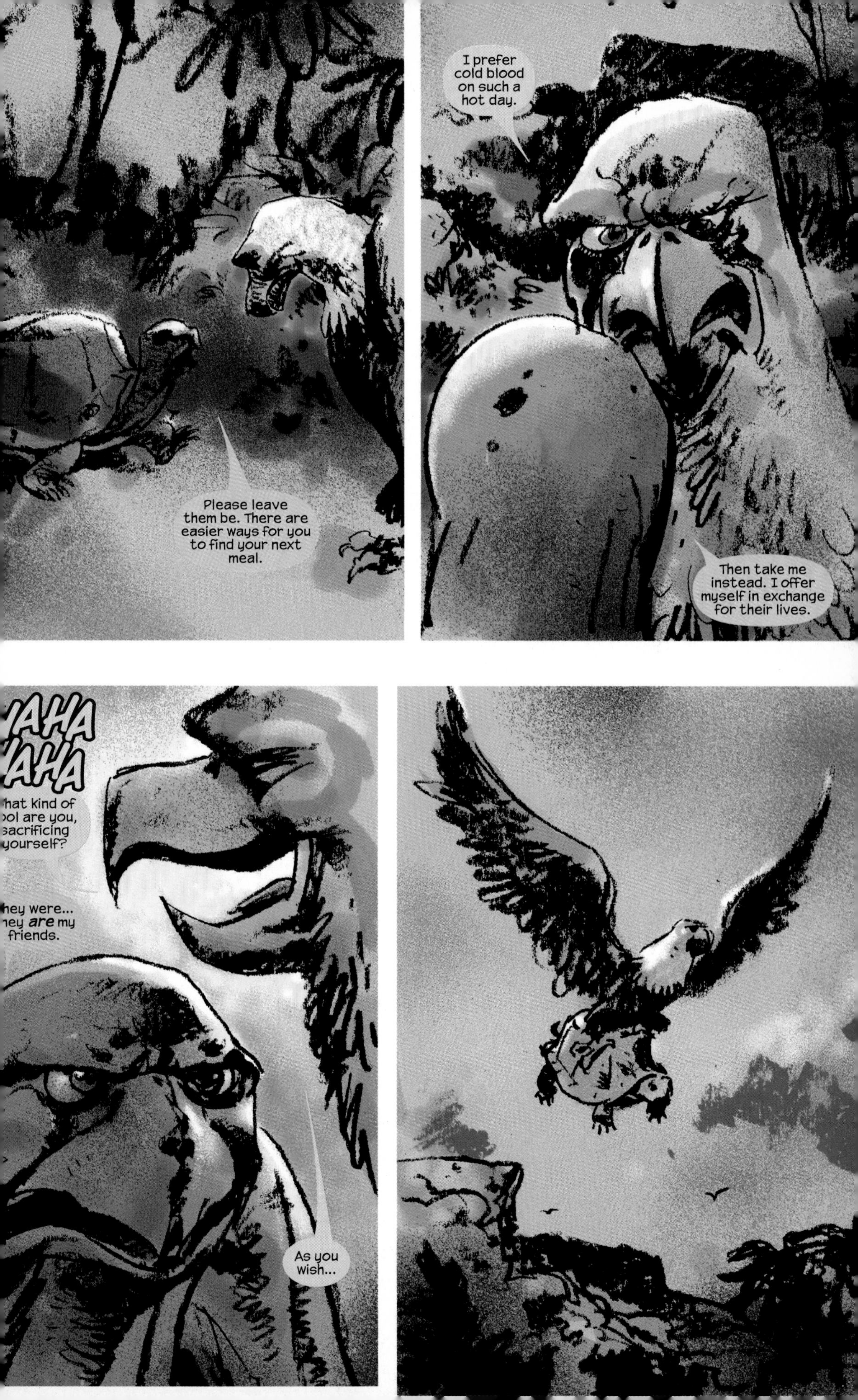
Please leave them be. There are easier ways for you to find your next meal.
I prefer cold blood on such a hot day.
Then take me instead. I offer myself in exchange for their lives.
IAHA IAHA
hat kind of ool are you, sacrificing yourself?
hey were... ey *are* my friends.
As you wish...

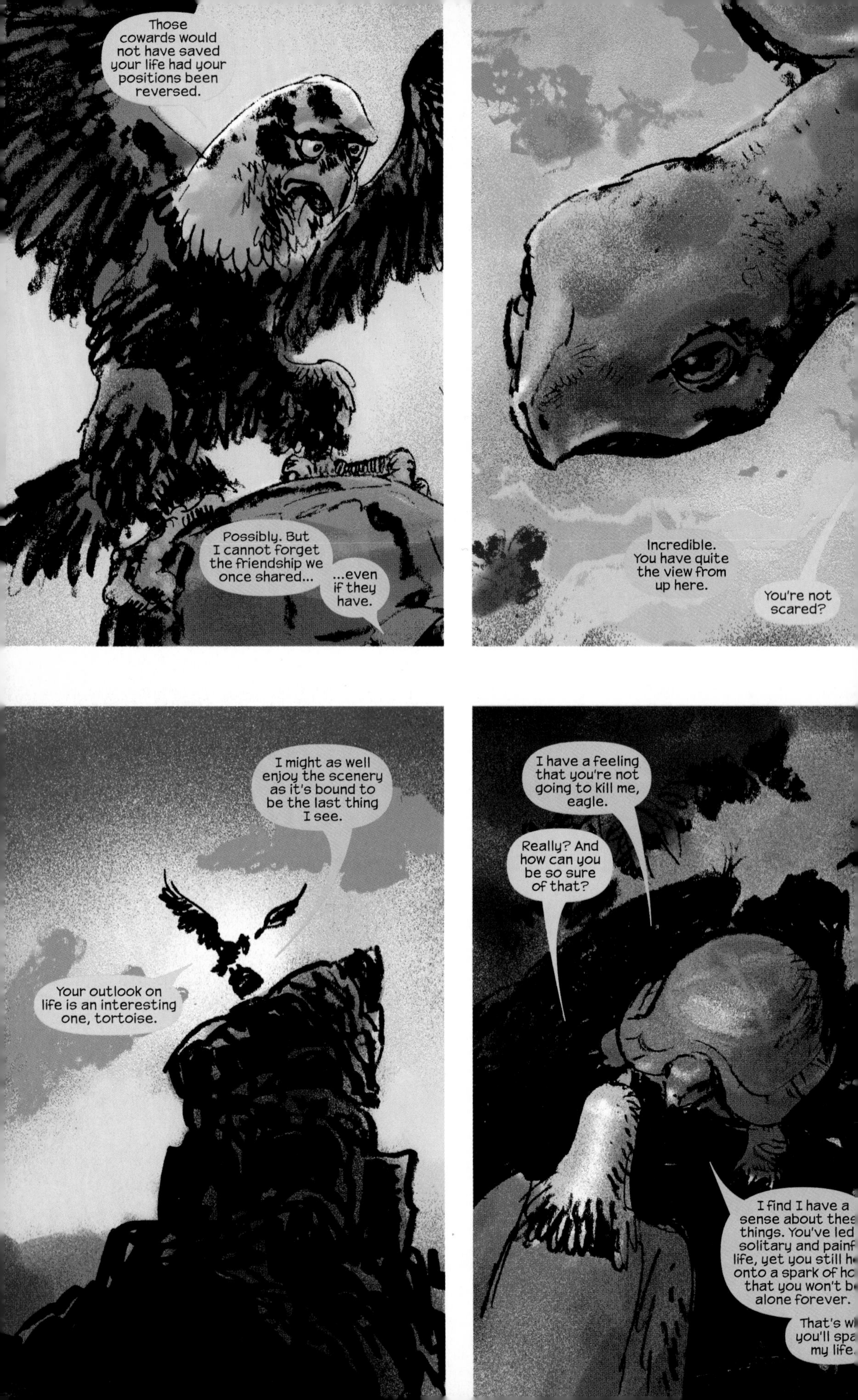
Those cowards would not have saved your life had your positions been reversed.
Possibly. But I cannot forget the friendship we once shared...
...even if they have.
Incredible. You have quite the view from up here.
You're not scared?
I might as well enjoy the scenery as it's bound to be the last thing I see.
Your outlook on life is an interesting one, tortoise.
I have a feeling that you're not going to kill me, eagle.
Really? And how can you be so sure of that?
I find I have a sense about thes things. You've led solitary and painf life, yet you still h onto a spark of ho that you won't b alone forever.
That's w you'll spa my life

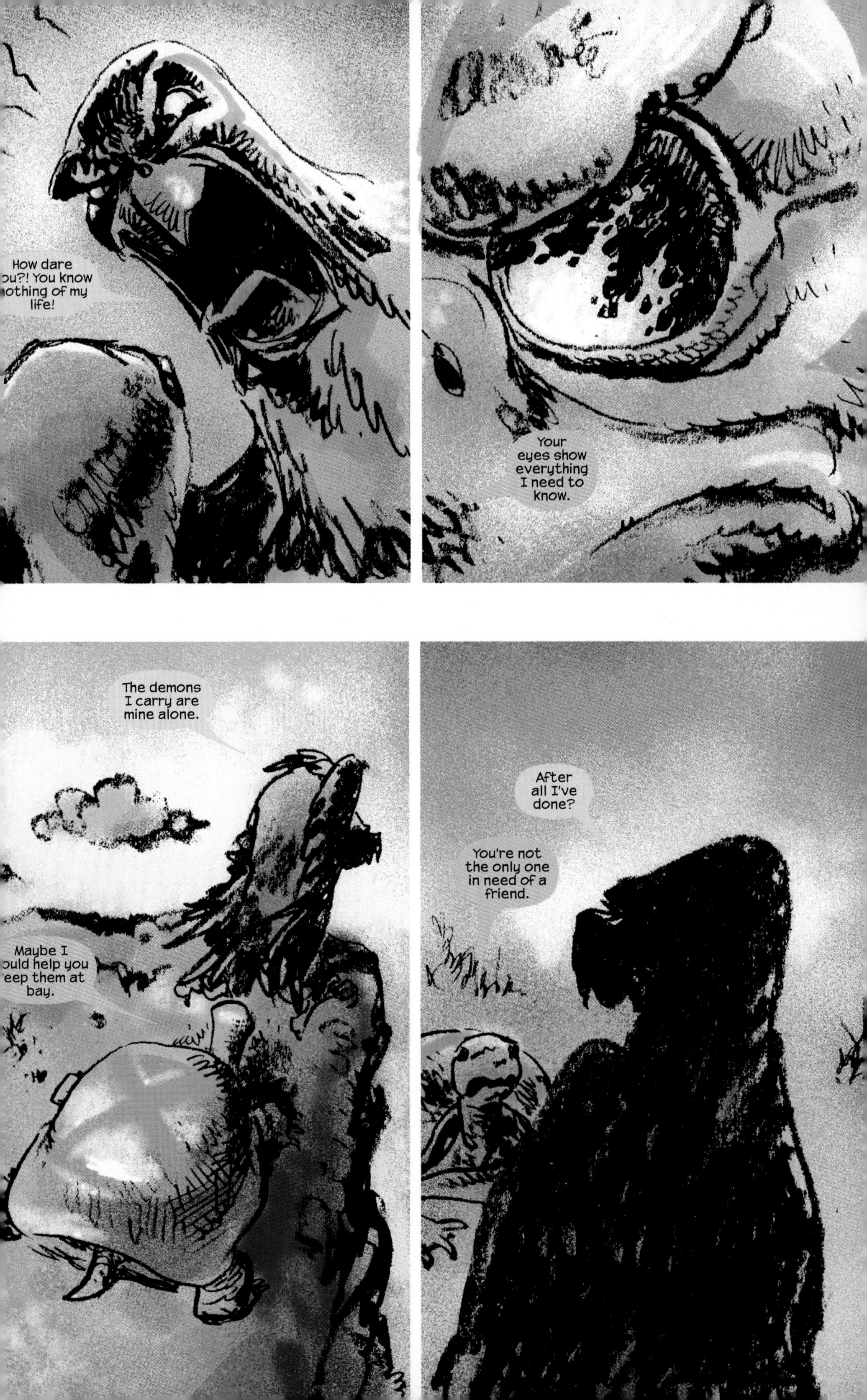
How dare ou?! You know othing of my life!
Your eyes show everything I need to know.
The demons I carry are mine alone.
Maybe I ould help you eep them at bay.
After all I've done?
You're not the only one in need of a friend.

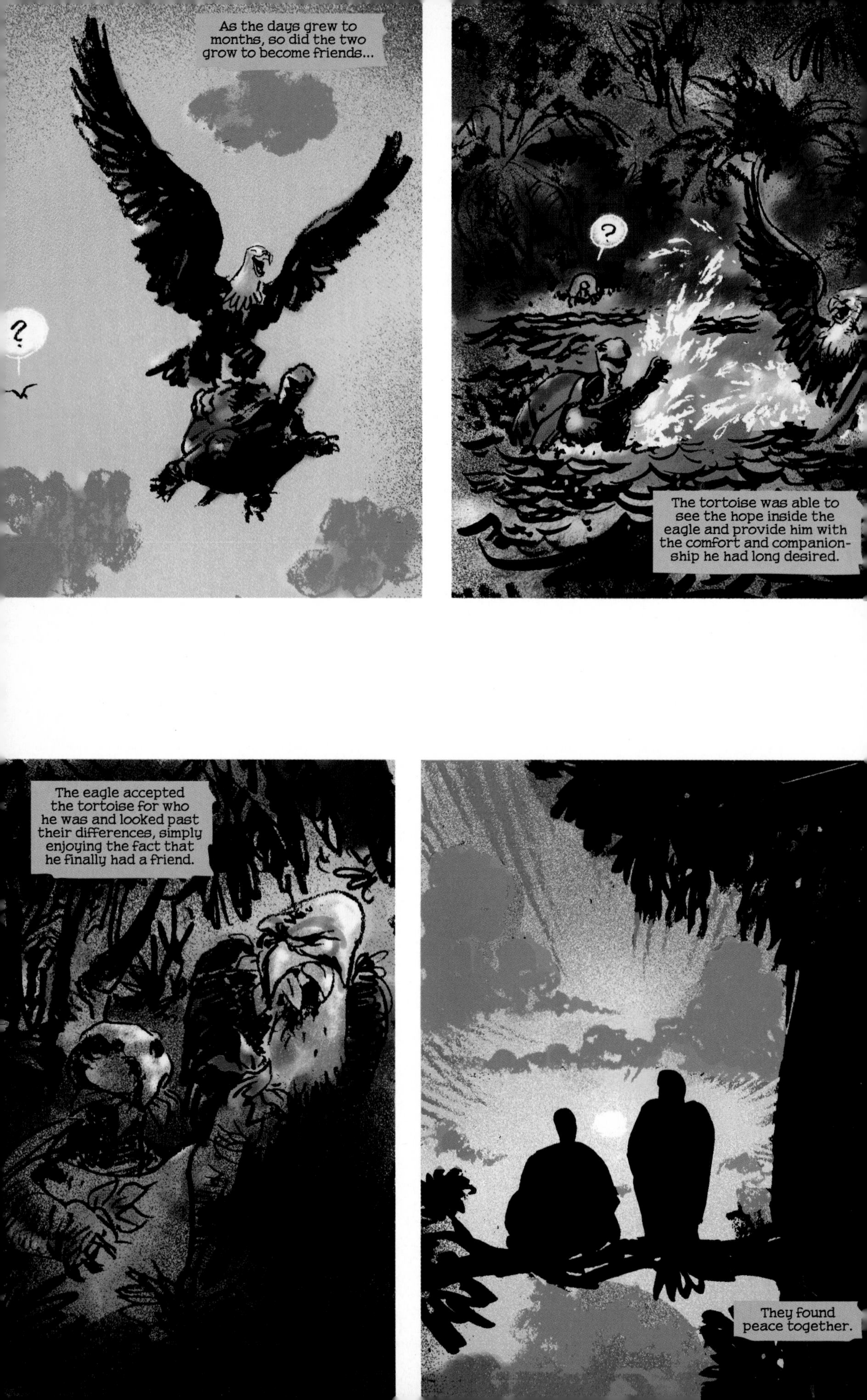
As the days grew to months, so did the two grow to become friends...
?
?
The tortoise was able to see the hope inside the eagle and provide him with the comfort and companionship he had long desired.
The eagle accepted the tortoise for who he was and looked past their differences, simply enjoying the fact that he finally had a friend.
They found peace together.

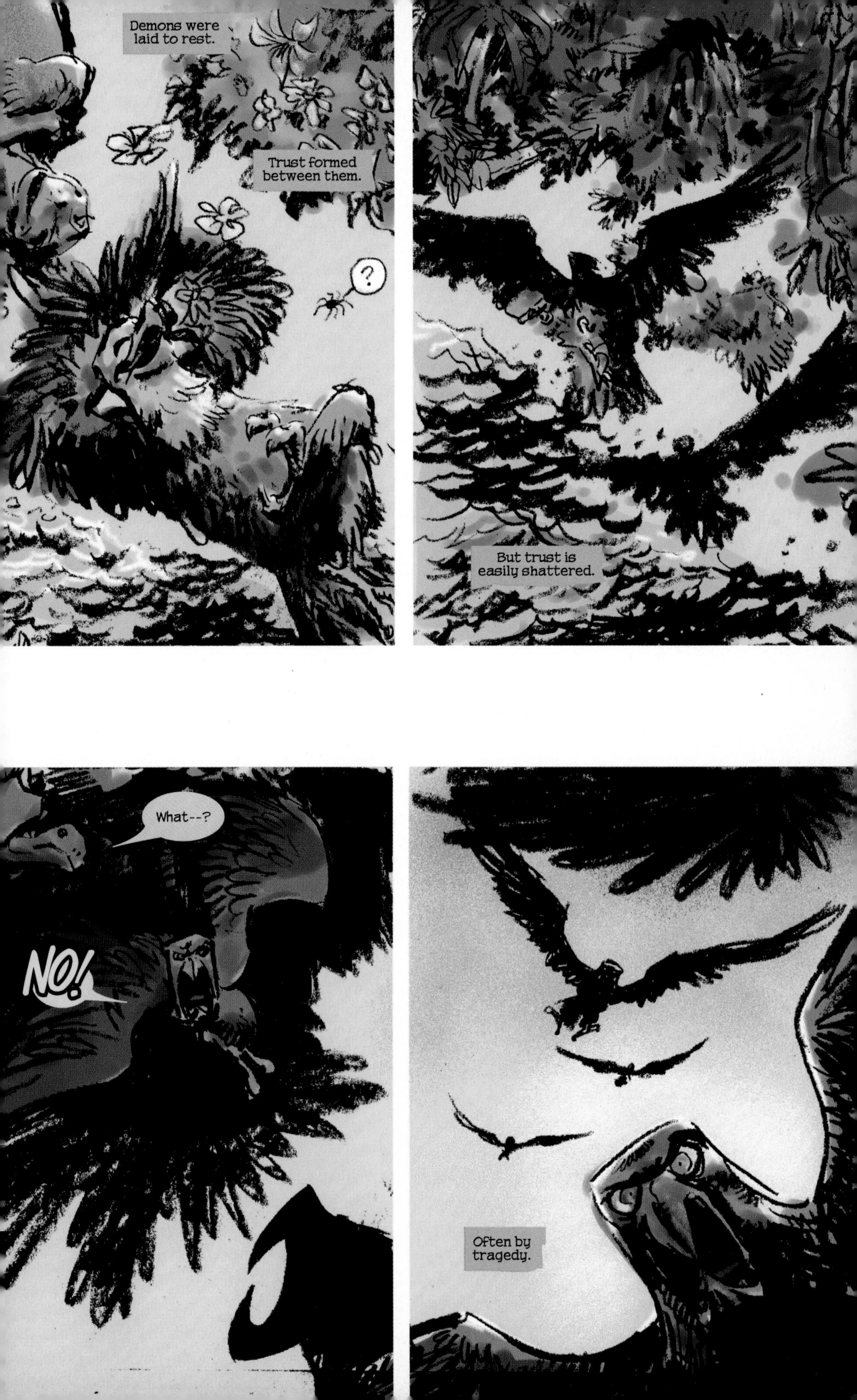
Demons were laid to rest.
Trust formed between them.
?
But trust is easily shattered.
What--?
NO!
Often by tragedy.

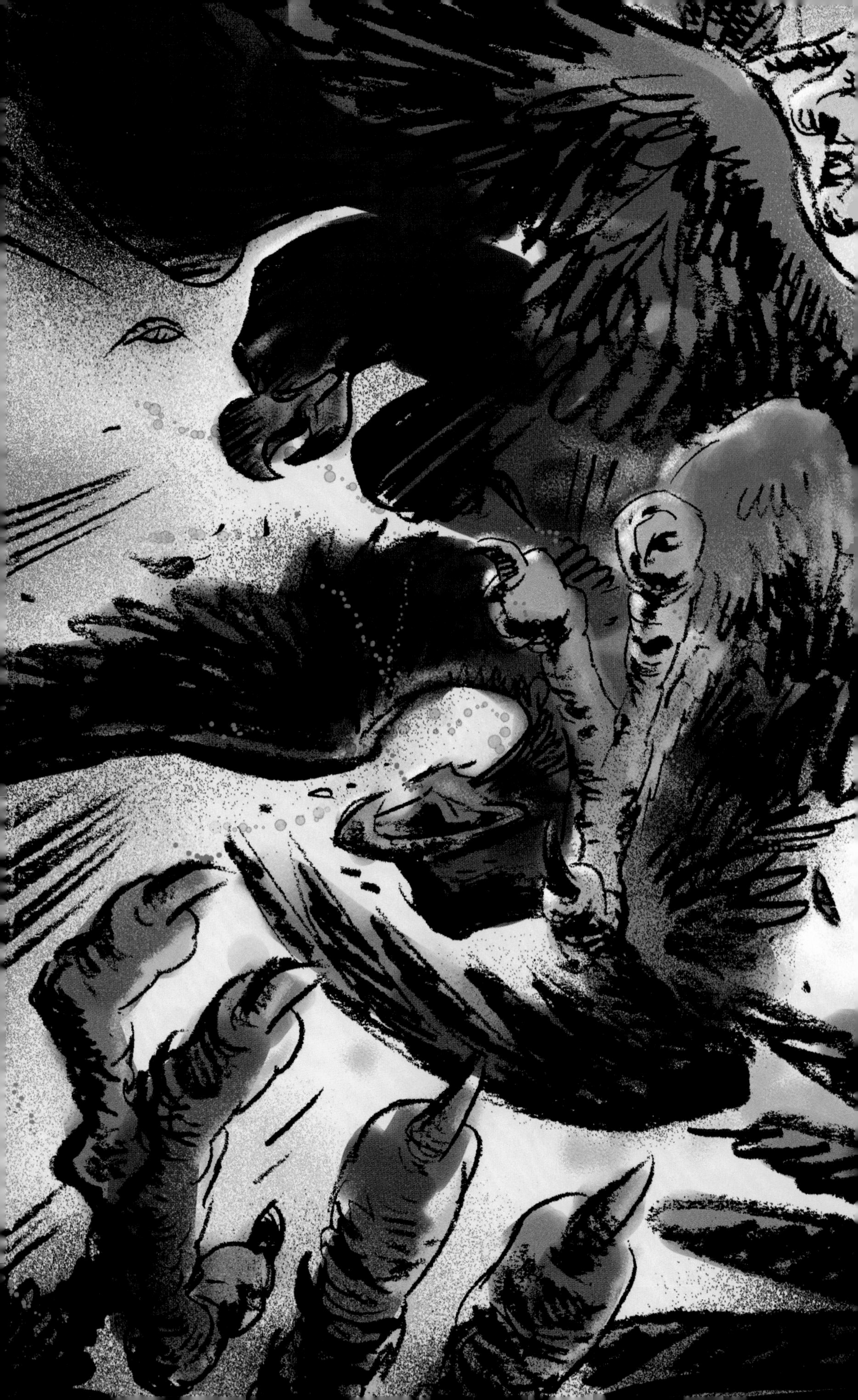

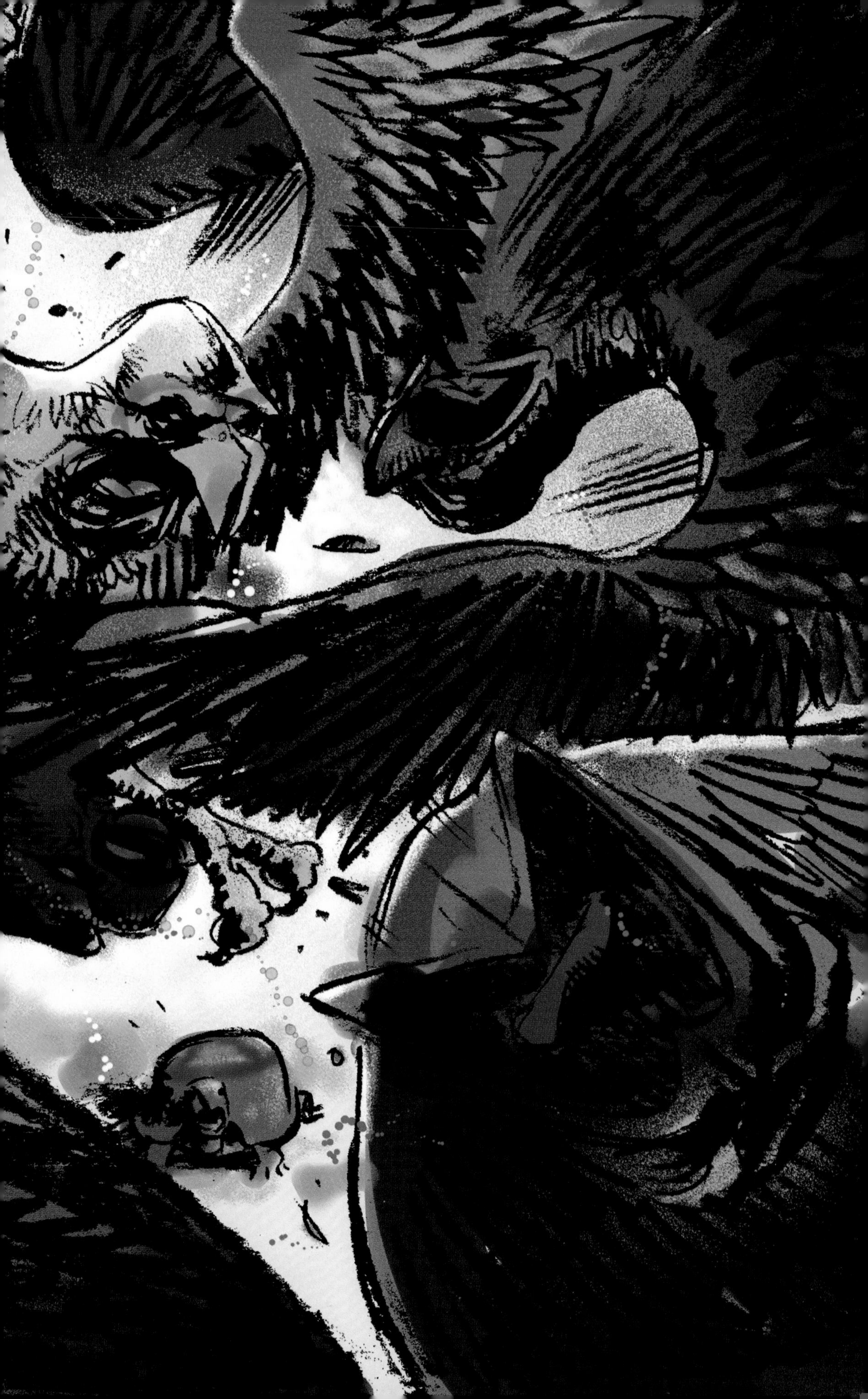

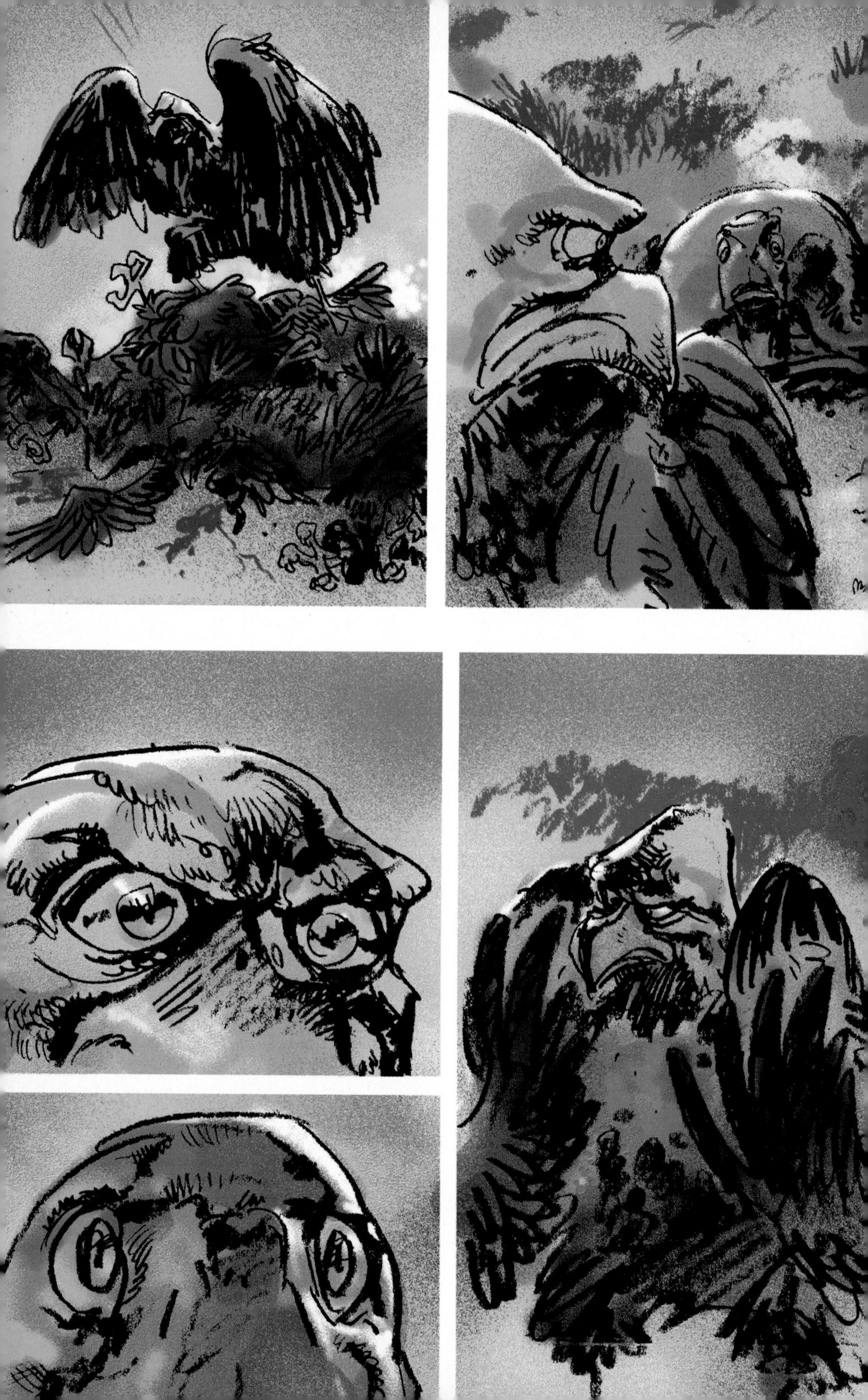

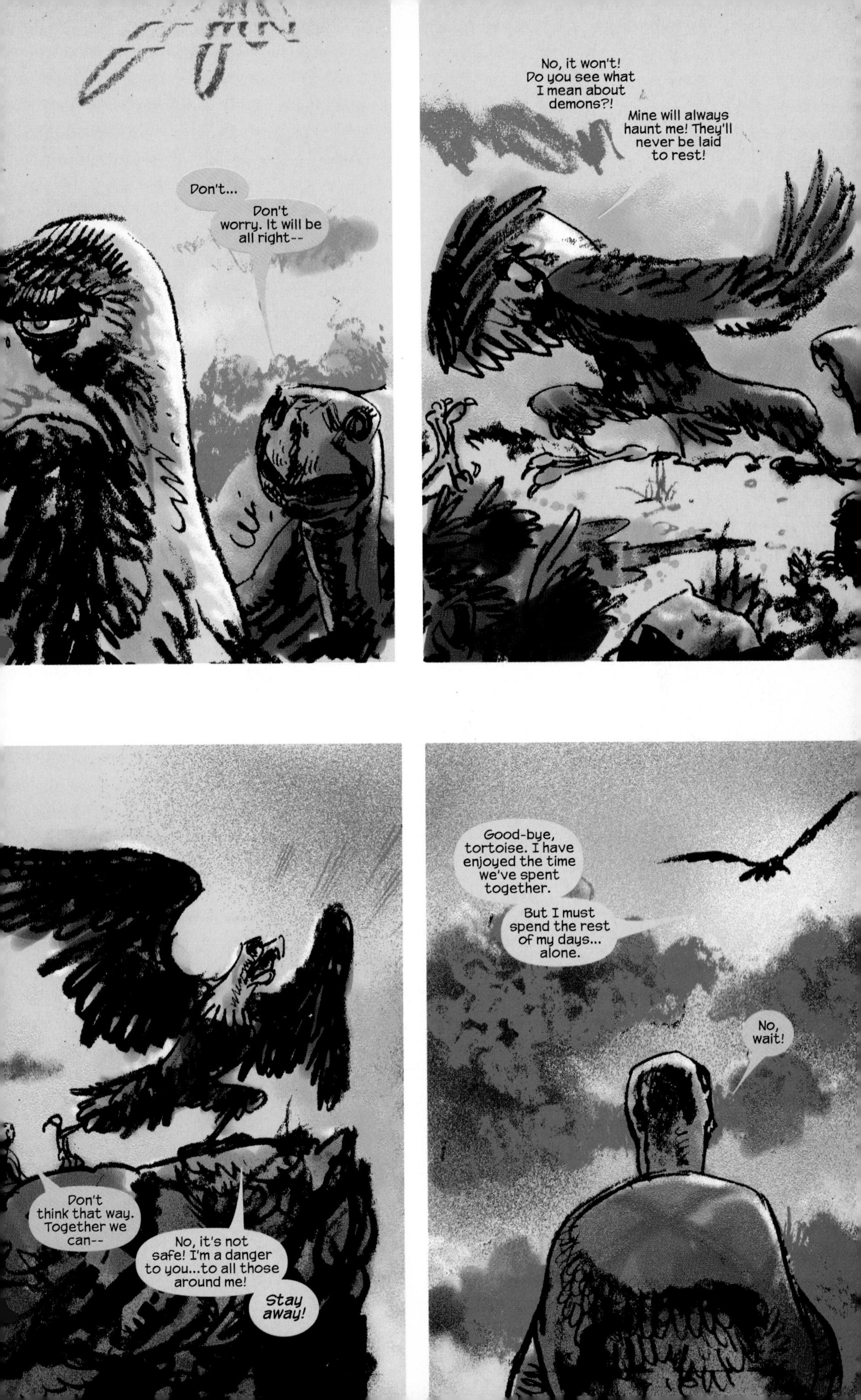
Don't...
Don't worry. It will be all right--
No, it won't! Do you see what I mean about demons?!
Mine will always haunt me! They'll never be laid to rest!
Don't think that way. Together we can--
No, it's not safe! I'm a danger to you...to all those around me!
Stay away!
Good-bye, tortoise. I have enjoyed the time we've spent together.
But I must spend the rest of my days... alone.
No, wait!

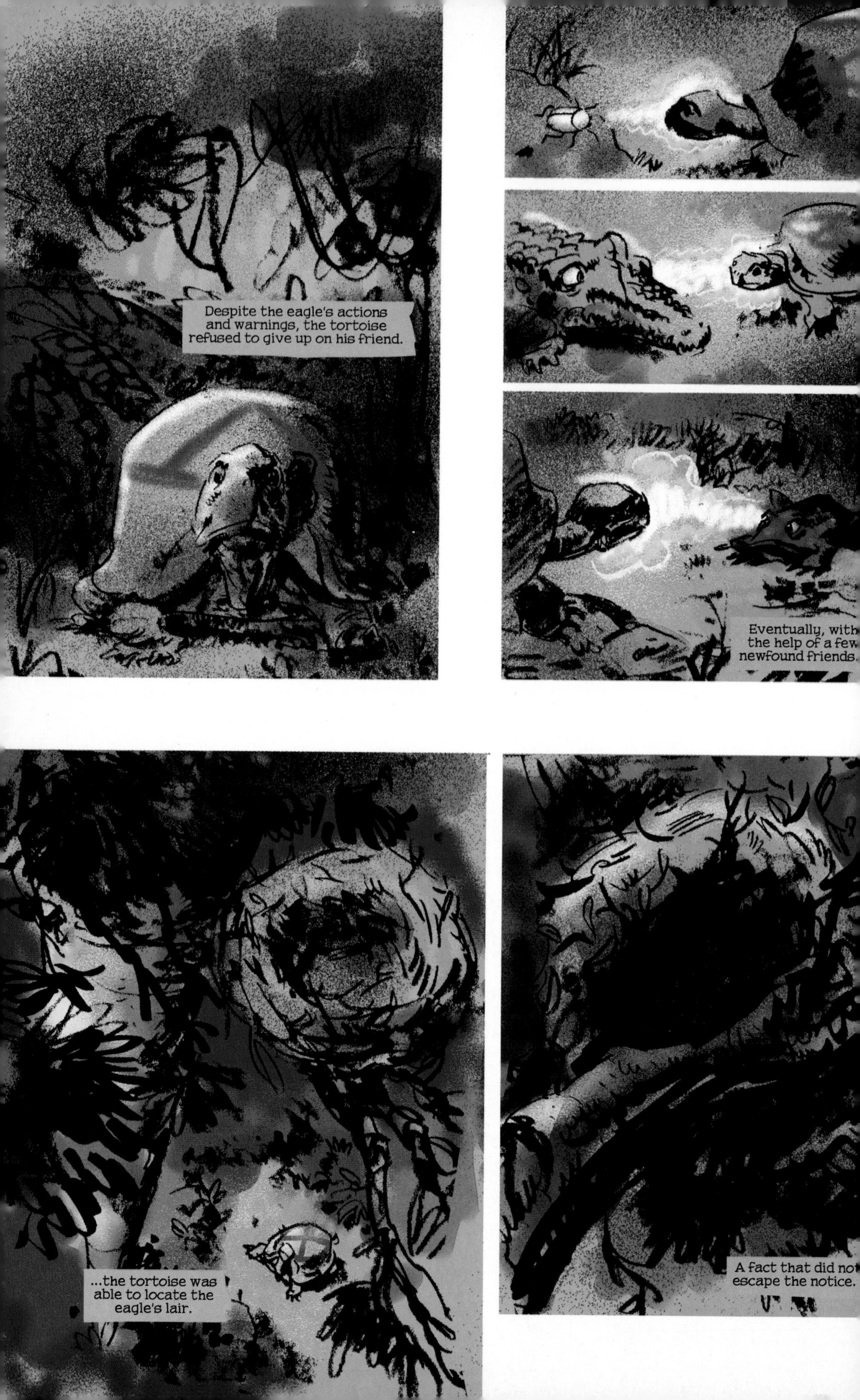
Despite the eagle's actions and warnings, the tortoise refused to give up on his friend.
Eventually, with the help of a few newfound friends...
...the tortoise was able to locate the eagle's lair.
A fact that did no
escape the notice.

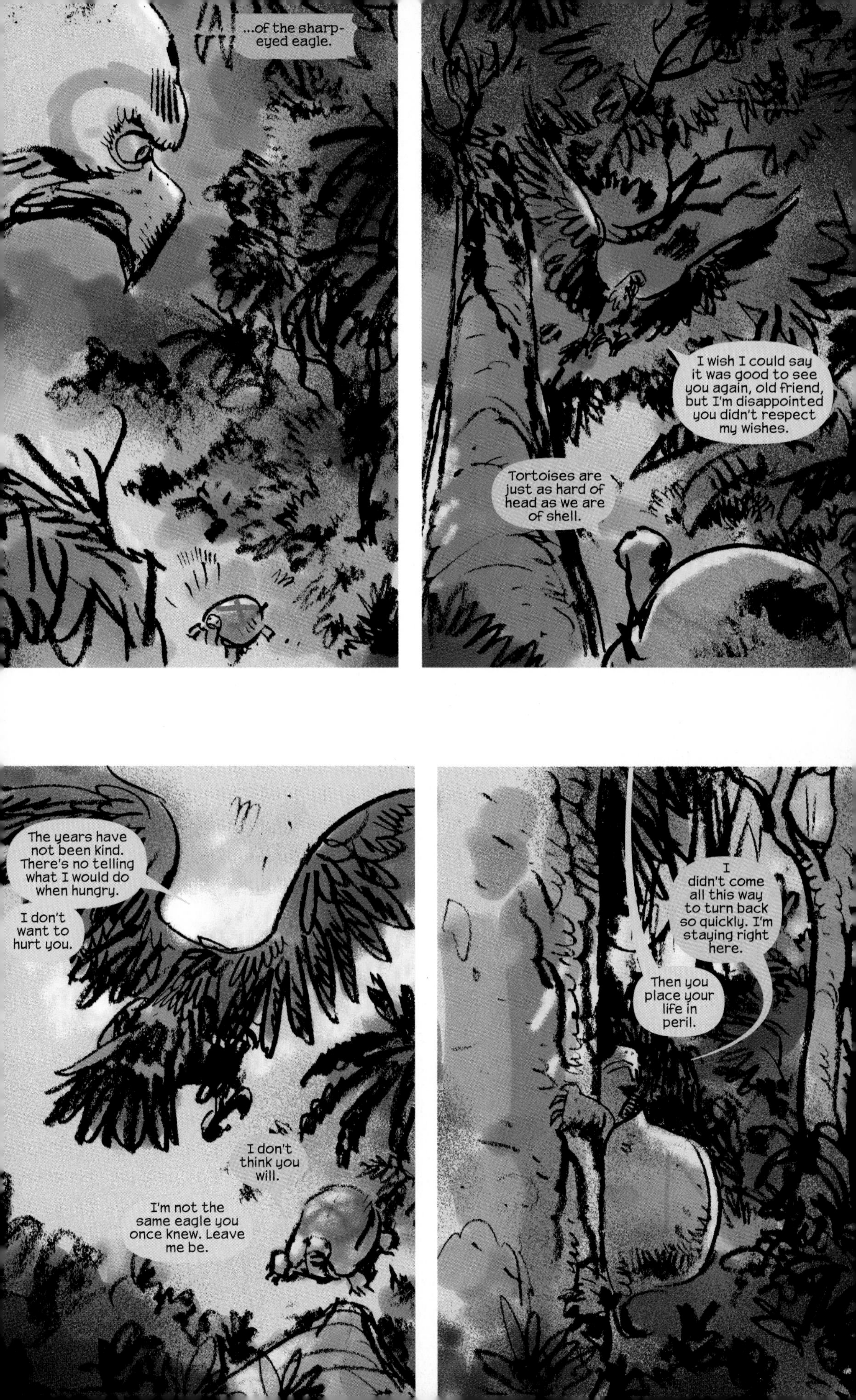
...of the sharp-eyed eagle.
I wish I could say it was good to see you again, old friend, but I'm disappointed you didn't respect my wishes.
Tortoises are just as hard of head as we are of shell.
The years have not been kind. There's no telling what I would do when hungry.
I don't want to hurt you.
I don't think you will.
I'm not the same eagle you once knew. Leave me be.
I didn't come all this way to turn back so quickly. I'm staying right here.
Then you place your life in peril.

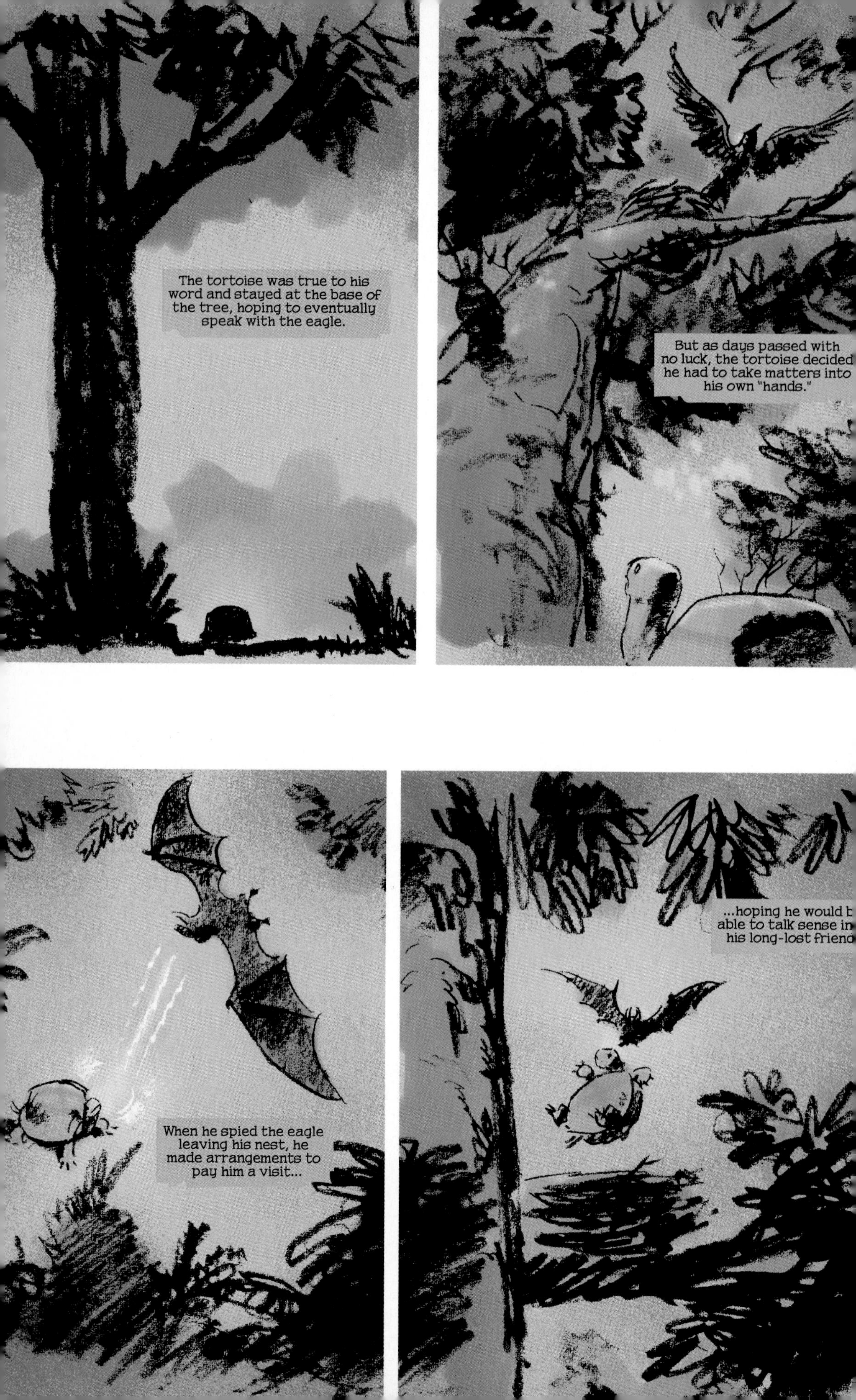
The tortoise was true to his word and stayed at the base of the tree, hoping to eventually speak with the eagle.
But as days passed with no luck, the tortoise decided he had to take matters into his own "hands."
When he spied the eagle leaving his nest, he made arrangements to pay him a visit...
...hoping he would b able to talk sense in his long-lost friend

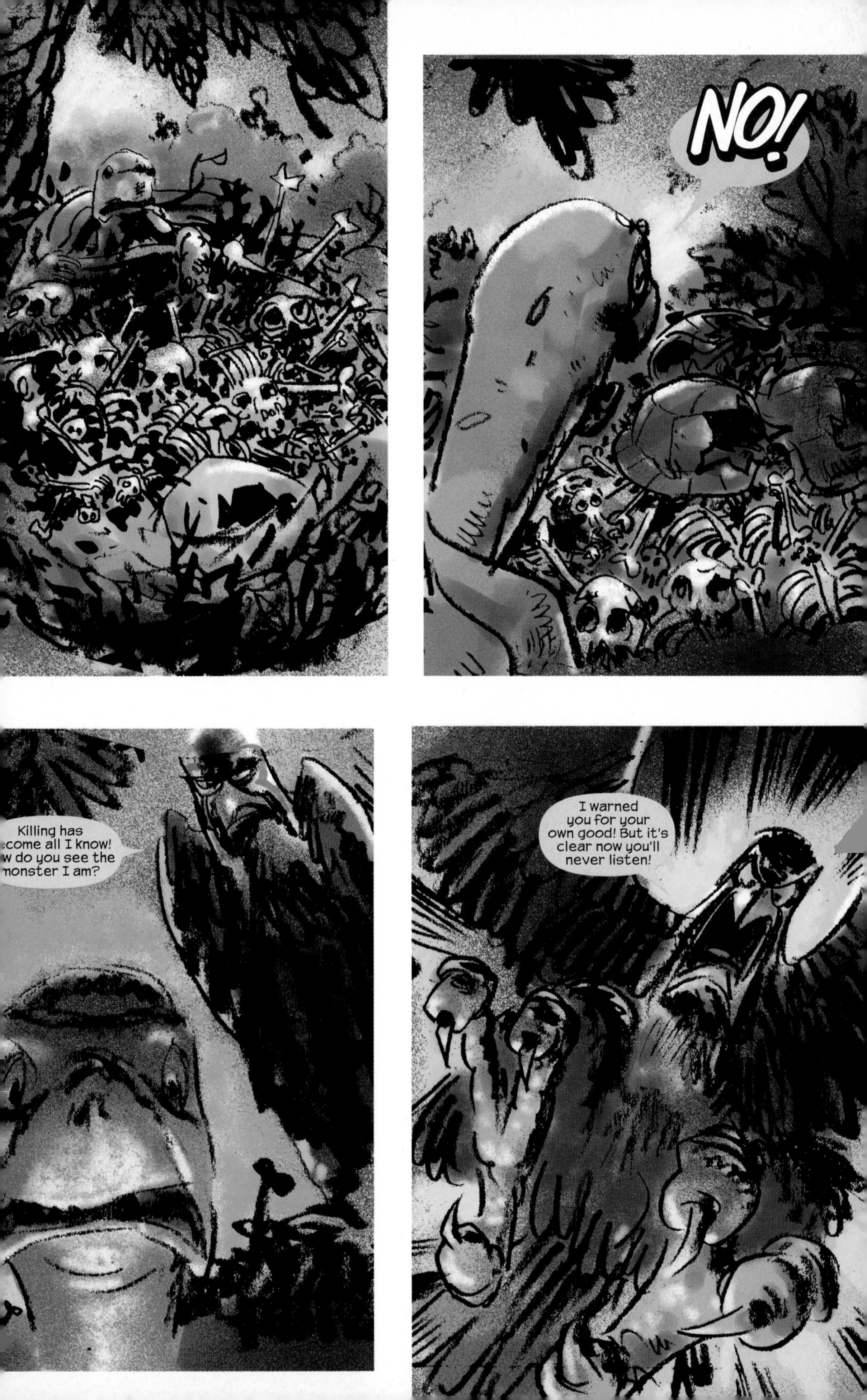
NO!
Killing has come all I know! w do you see the monster I am?
I warned you for your own good! But it's clear now you'll never listen!

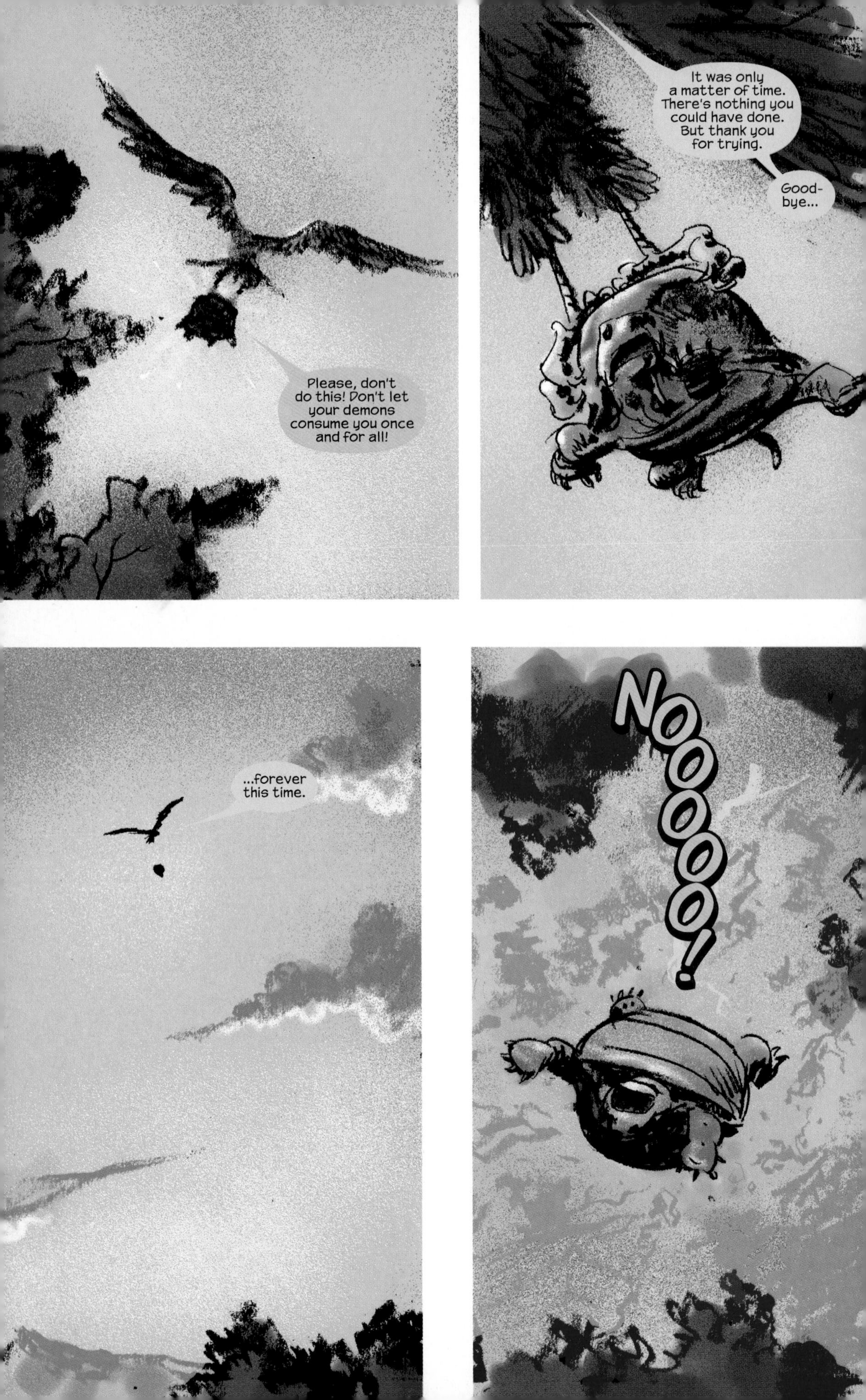
Please, don't do this! Don't let your demons consume you once and for all!
It was only a matter of time. There's nothing you could have done. But thank you for trying.
Good-bye...
...forever this time.
NOOOOO!

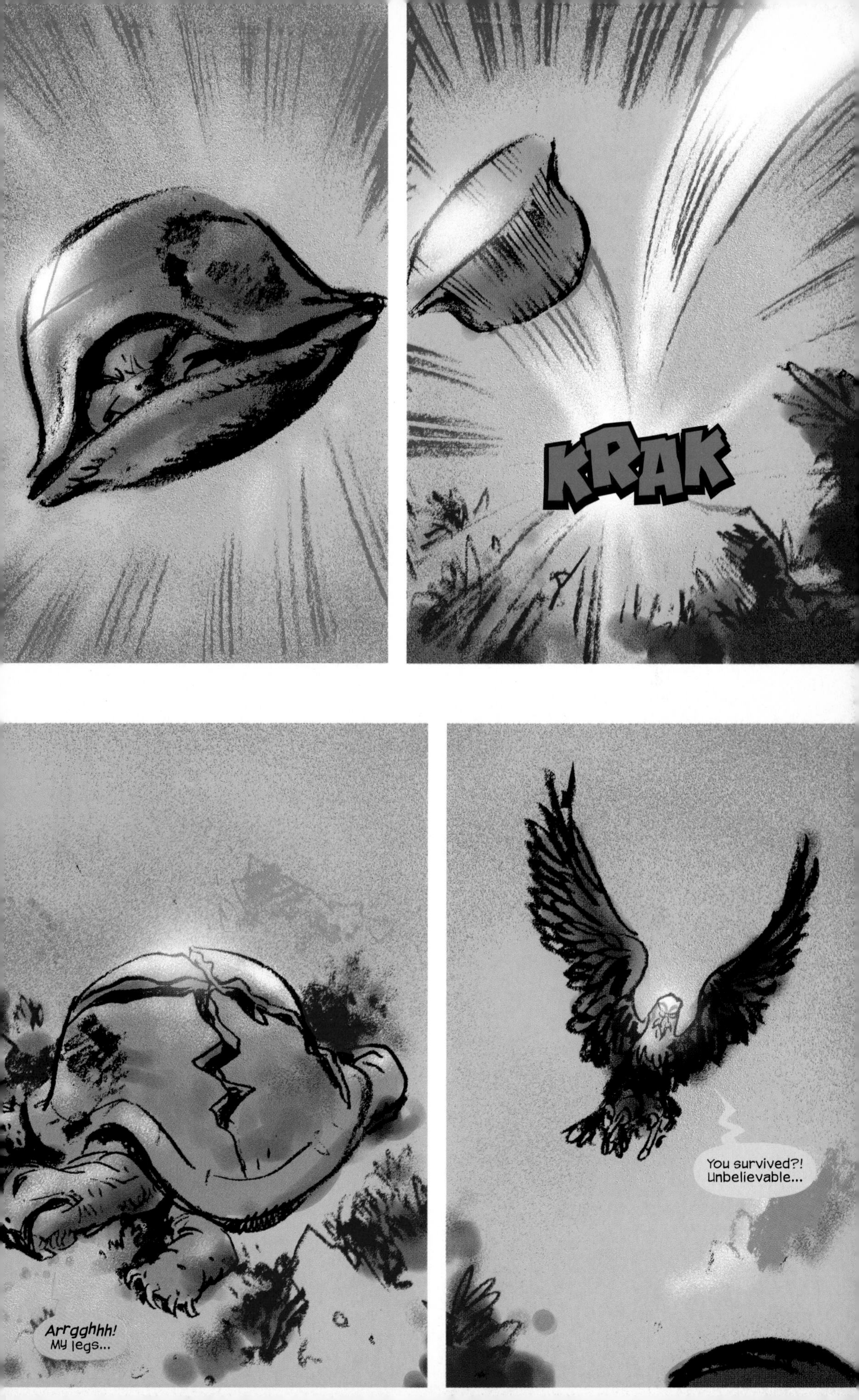
KRAK
Arrgghhh!
My legs...
You survived?!
Unbelievable...

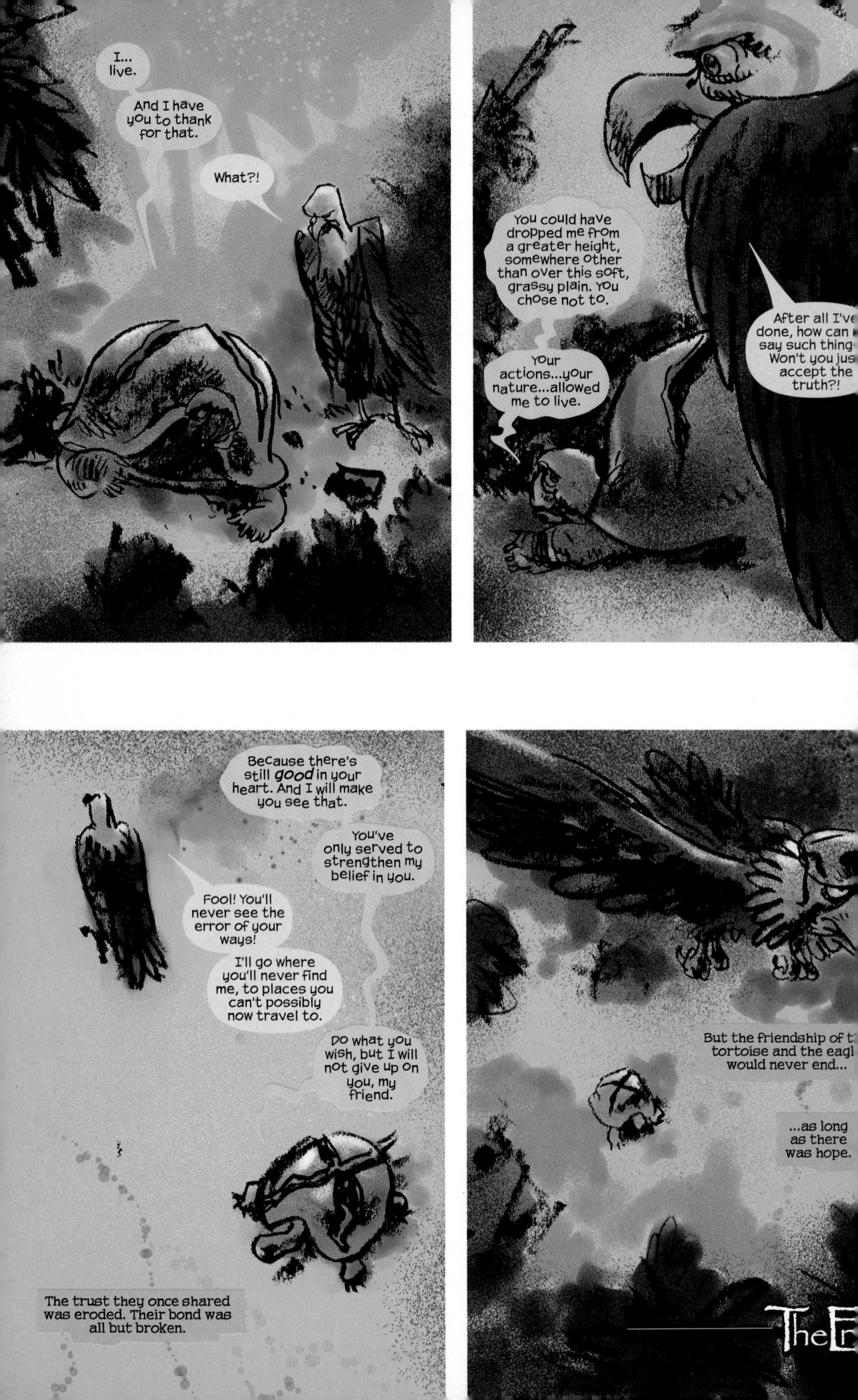
I... live.
And I have you to thank for that.
What?!
You could have dropped me from a greater height, somewhere other than over this soft, grassy plain. You chose not to.
Your actions...your nature...allowed me to live.
After all I've done, how can say such thing Won't you jus accept the truth?!
Because there's still *good* in your heart. And I will make you see that.
You've only served to strengthen my belief in you.
Fool! You'll never see the error of your ways!
I'll go where you'll never find me, to places you can't possibly now travel to.
Do what you wish, but I will not give up on you, my friend.
The trust they once shared was eroded. Their bond was all but broken.
But the friendship of t tortoise and the eagl would never end...
...as long as there was hope.

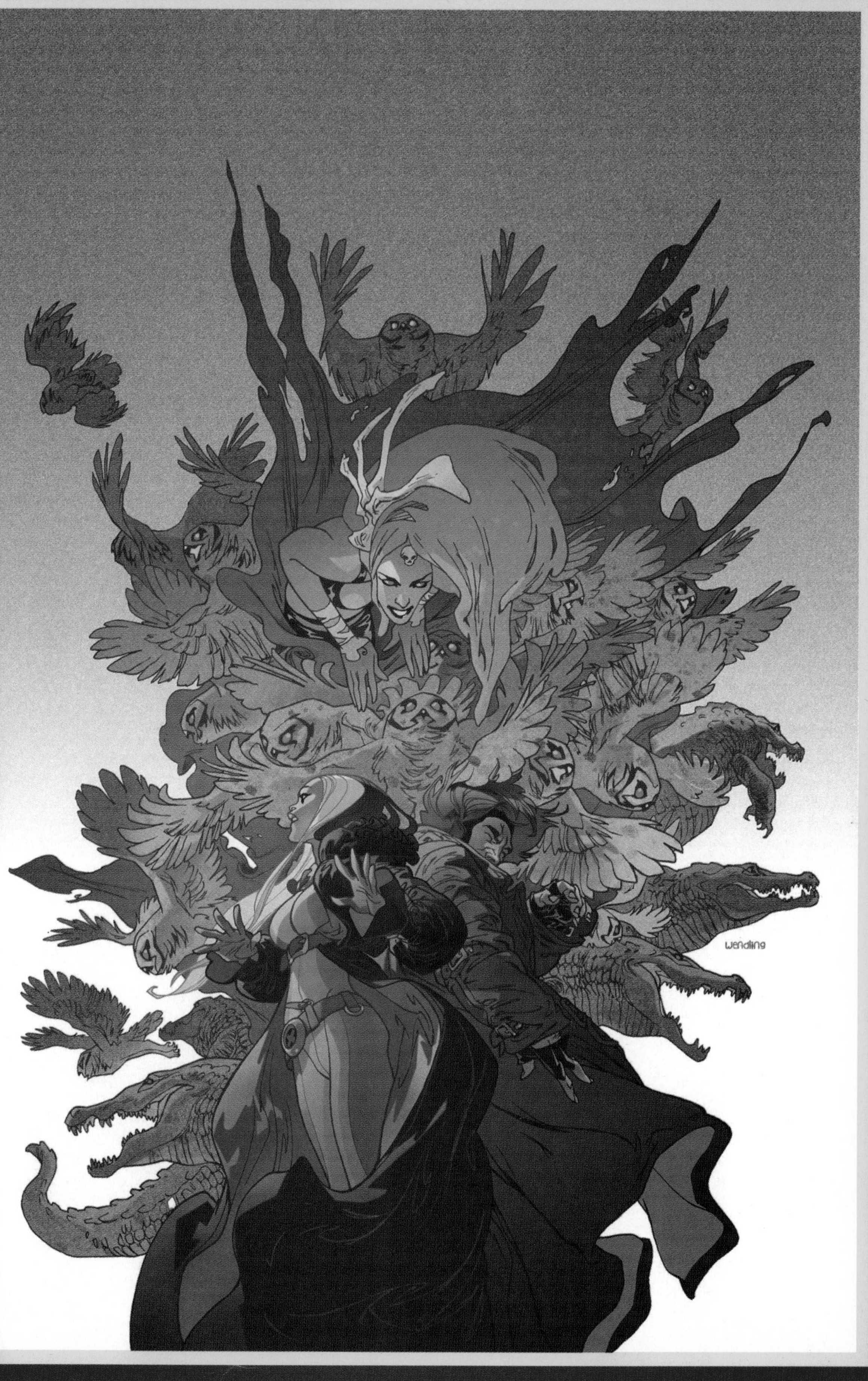
wendling

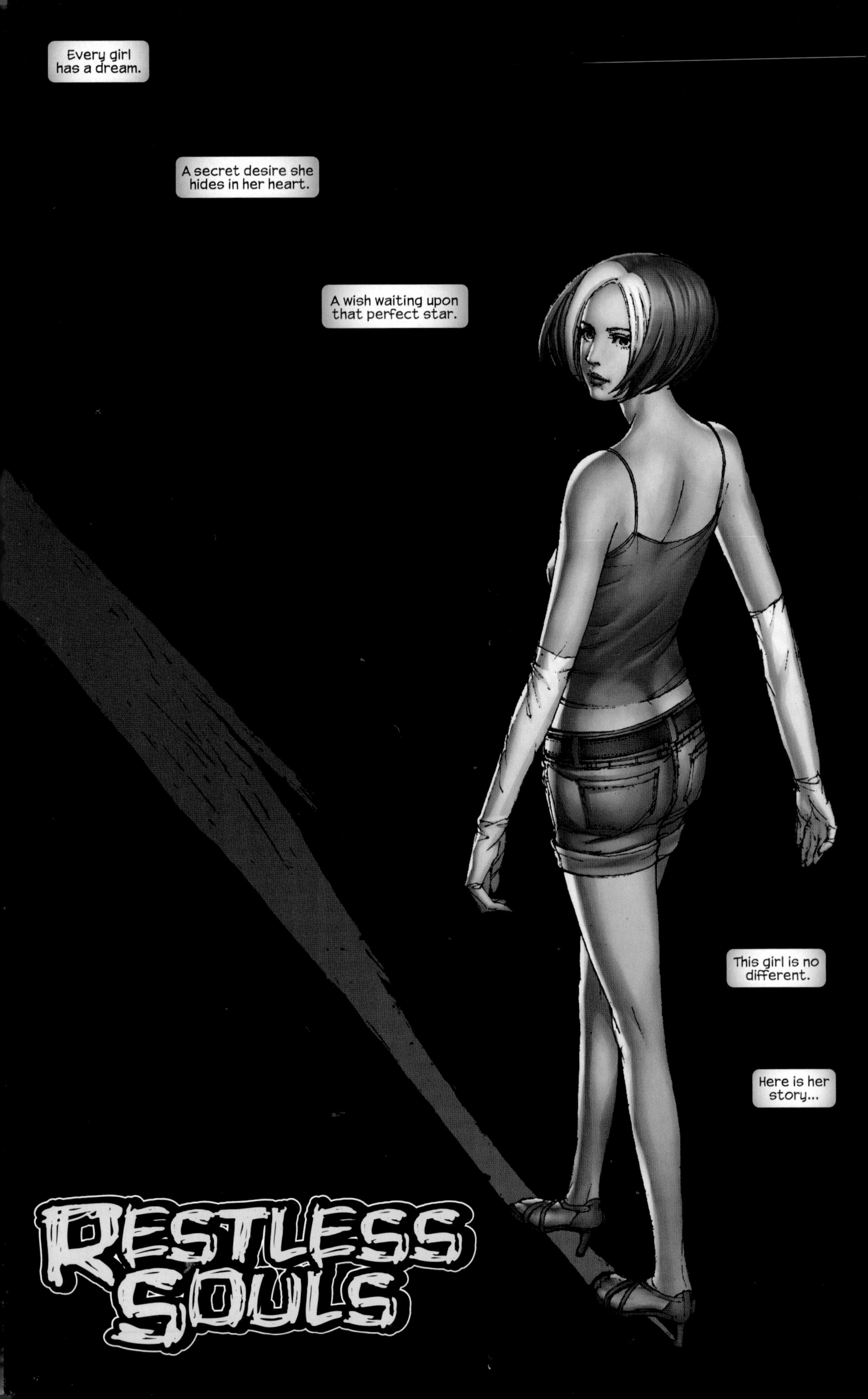
Every girl has a dream.
A secret desire she hides in her heart.
A wish waiting upon that perfect star.
This girl is no different.
Here is her story...
RESTLESS SOULS

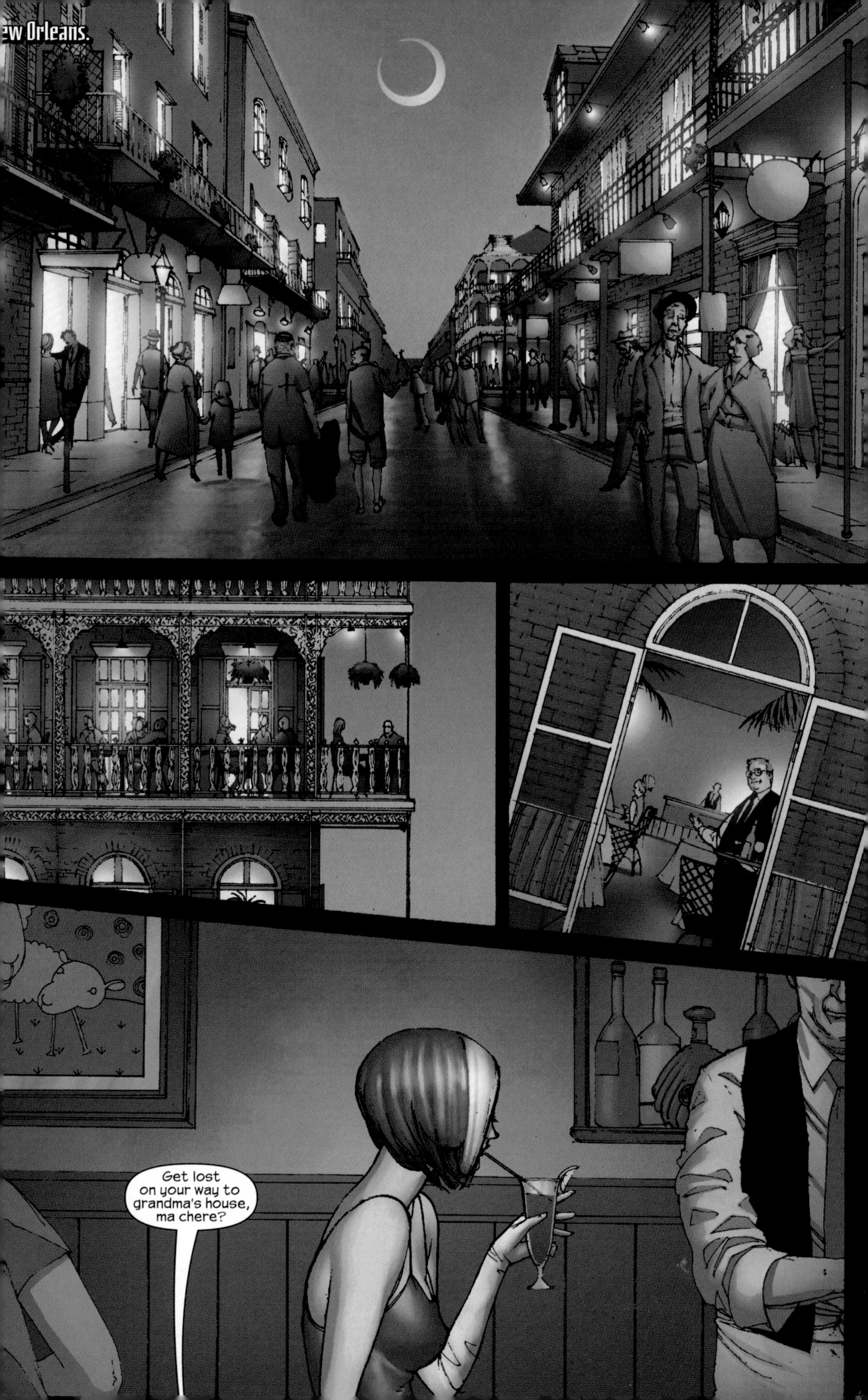
ew Orleans.
Get lost on your way to grandma's house, ma chere?

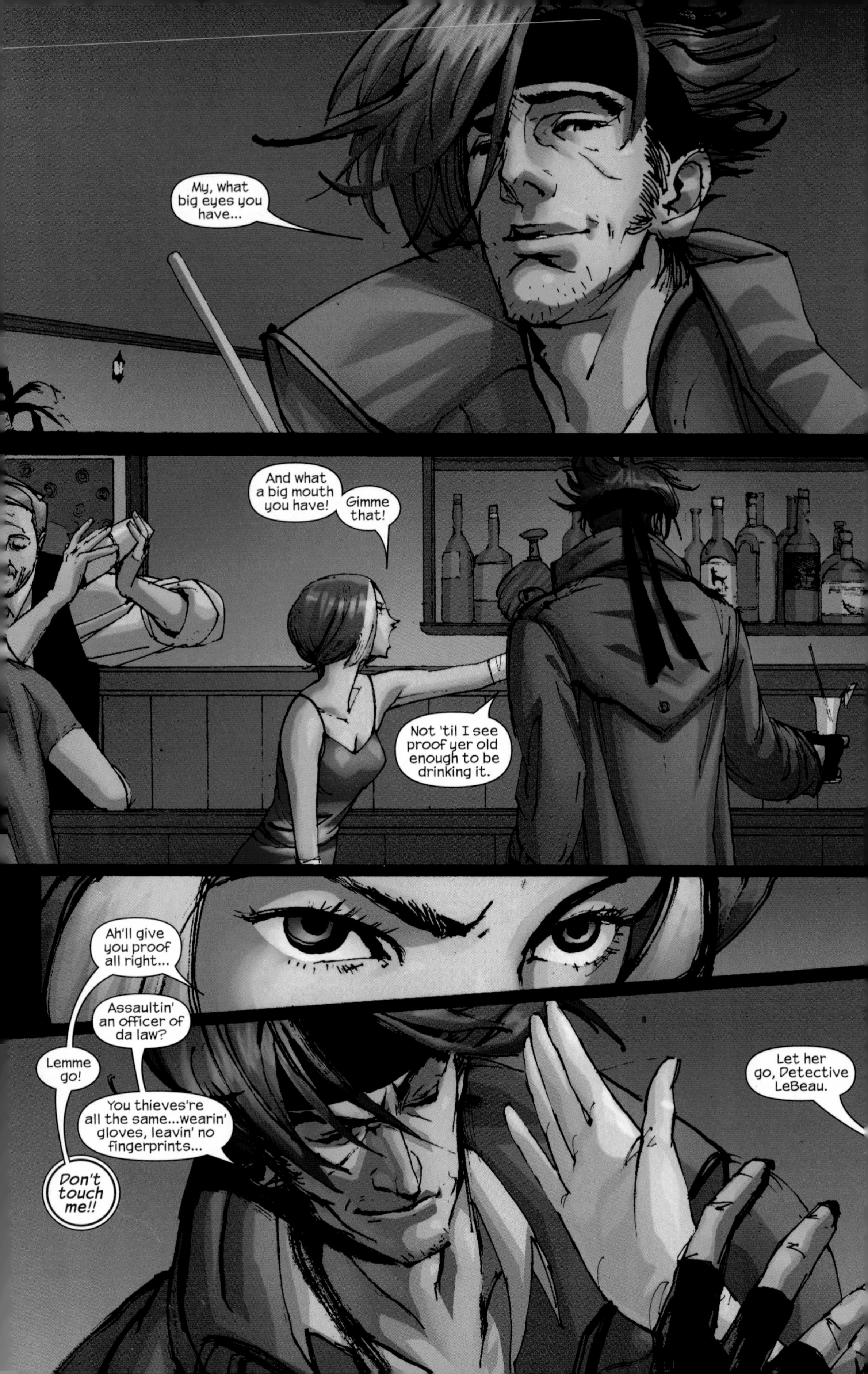

My, what big eyes you have...
And what a big mouth you have!
Gimme that!
Not 'til I see proof yer old enough to be drinking it.
Ah'll give you proof all right...
Assaultin' an officer of da law?
Lemme go!
You thieves're all the same...wearin' gloves, leavin' no fingerprints...
Don't touch me!!
Let her go, Detective LeBeau.

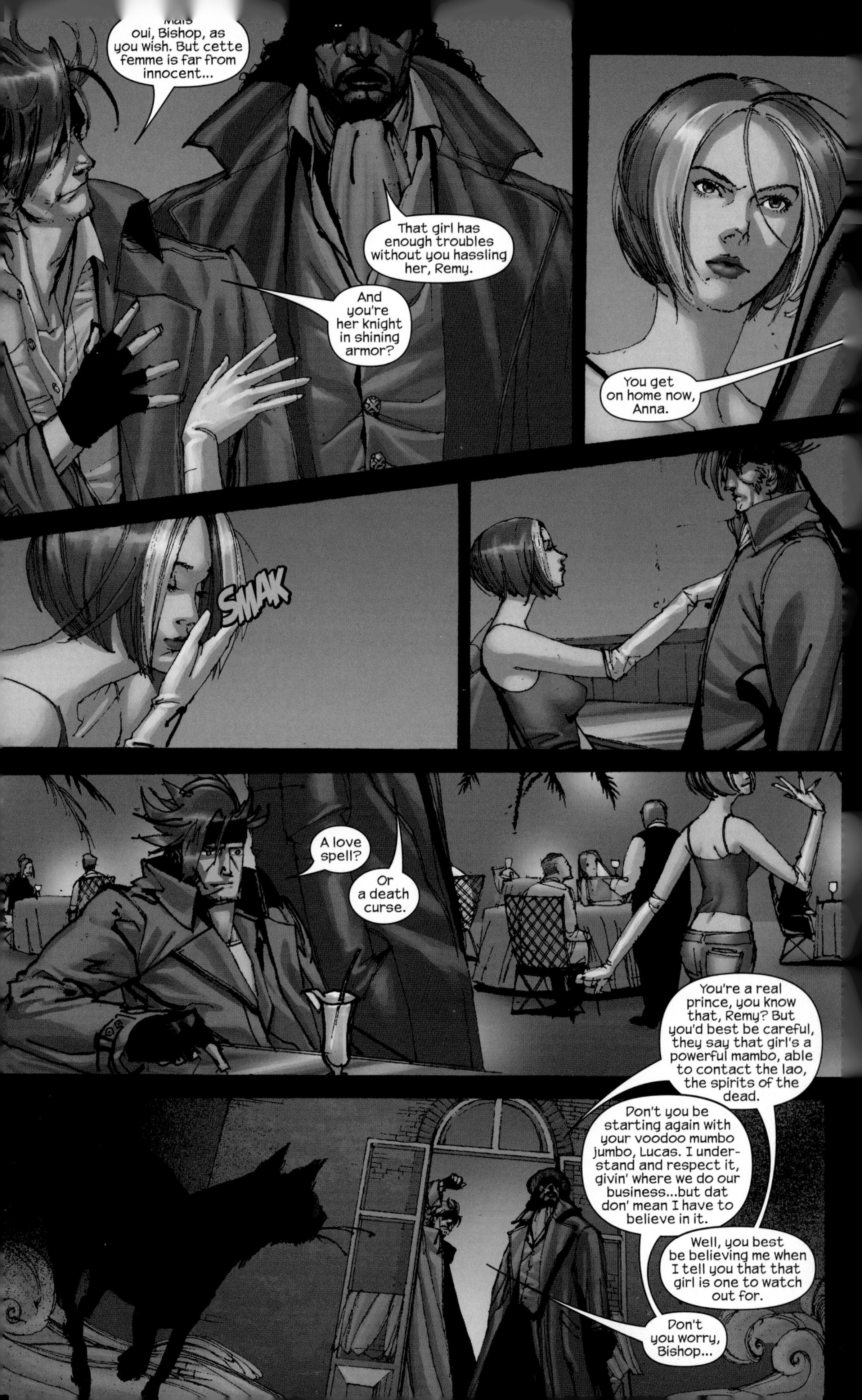

Mais oui, Bishop, as you wish. But cette femme is far from innocent...
That girl has enough troubles without you hassling her, Remy.
And you're her knight in shining armor?
You get on home now, Anna.
SMAK
A love spell?
Or a death curse.
You're a real prince, you know that, Remy? But you'd best be careful, they say that girl's a powerful mambo, able to contact the lao, the spirits of the dead.
Don't you be starting again with your voodoo mumbo jumbo, Lucas. I understand and respect it, givin' where we do our business...but dat don' mean I have to believe in it.
Well, you best be believing me when I tell you that that girl is one to watch out for.
Don't you worry, Bishop...

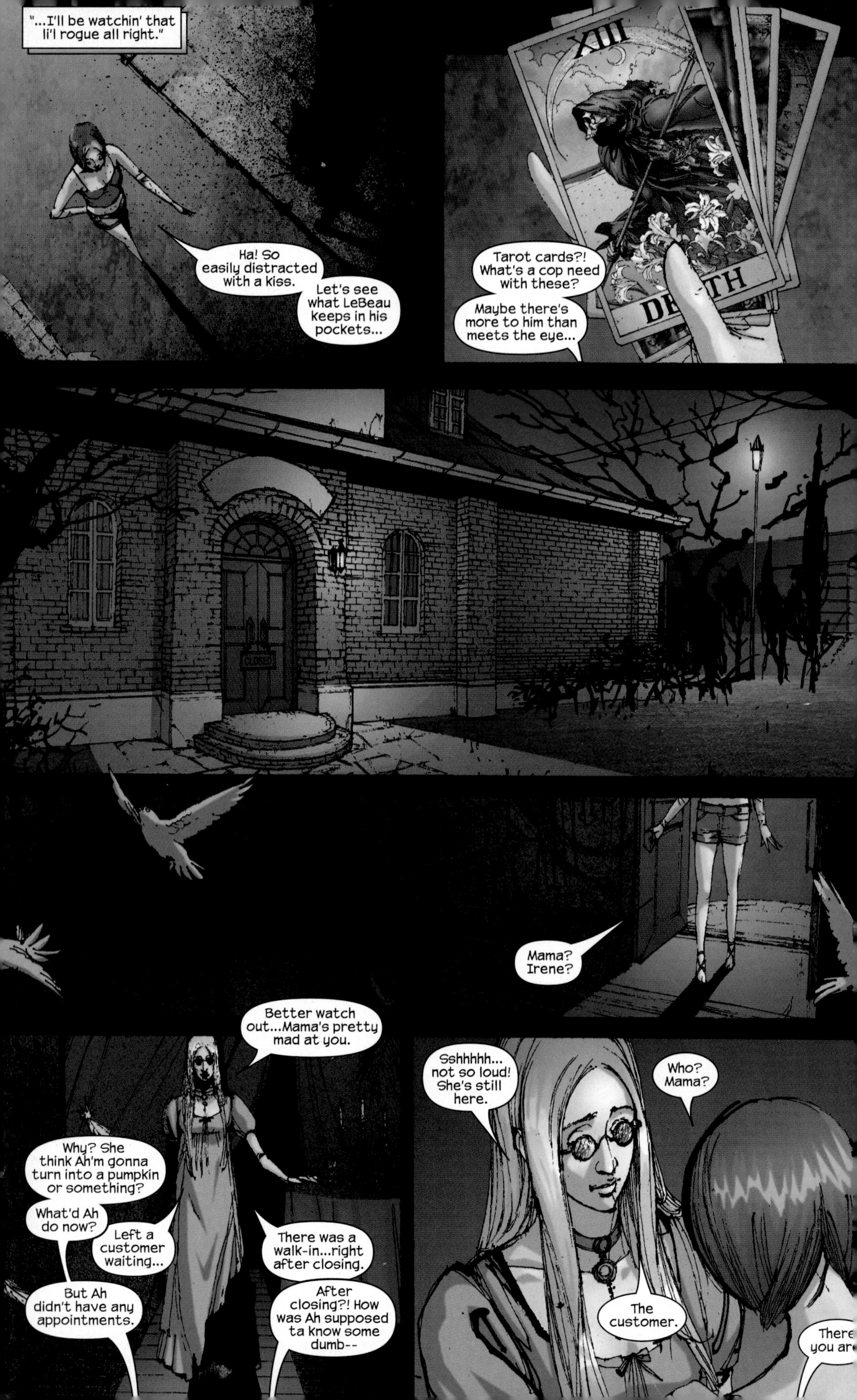
"...I'll be watchin' that li'l rogue all right."
Ha! So easily distracted with a kiss.
Let's see what LeBeau keeps in his pockets...
XIII
Tarot cards?! What's a cop need with these?
Maybe there's more to him than meets the eye...
CLOSED
Mama? Irene?
Better watch out...Mama's pretty mad at you.
Why? She think Ah'm gonna turn into a pumpkin or something?
What'd Ah do now?
Left a customer waiting...
But Ah didn't have any appointments.
There was a walk-in...right after closing.
After closing?! How was Ah supposed ta know some dumb--
Sshhhhh... not so loud! She's still here.
Who? Mama?
The customer.

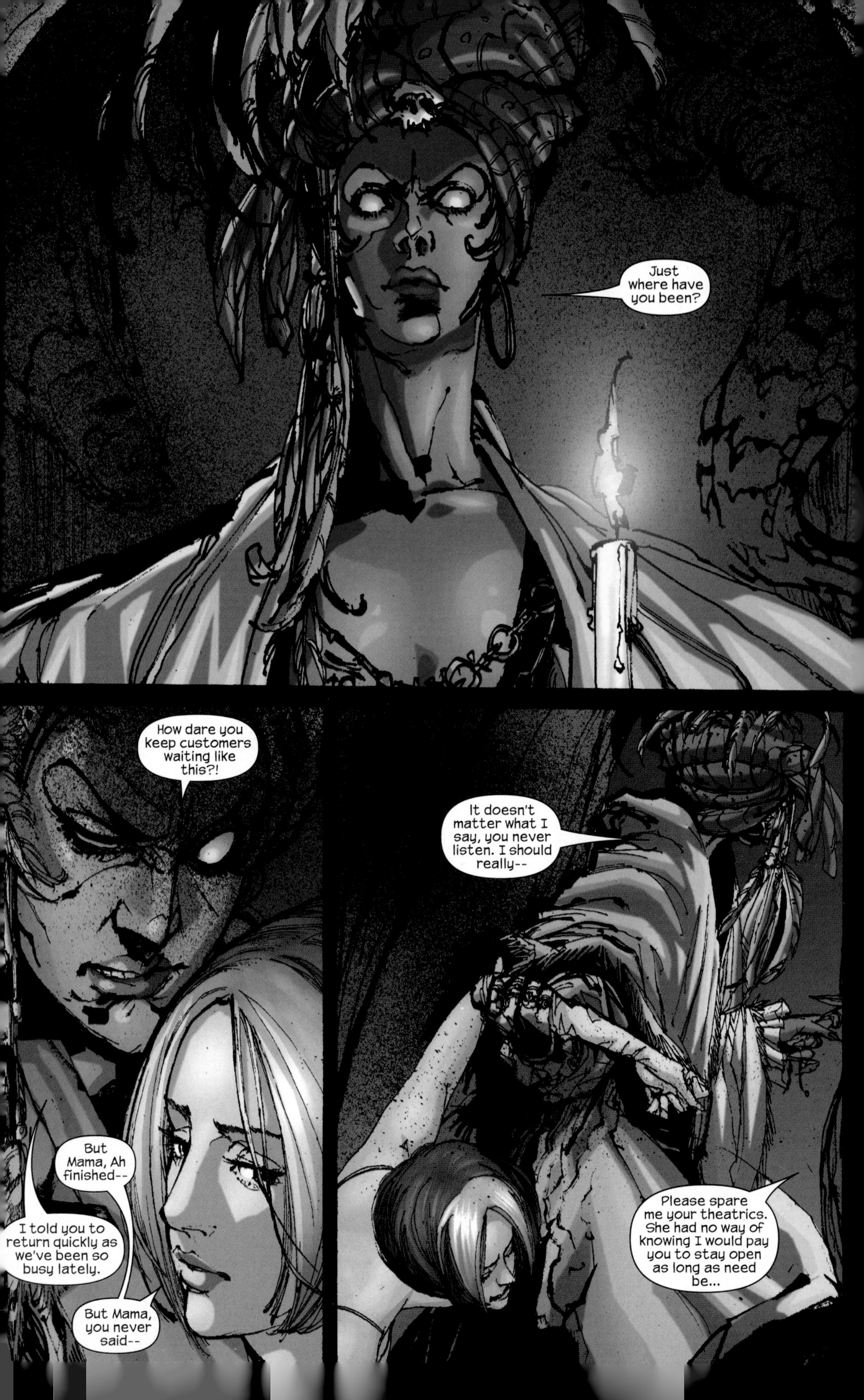
Just where have you been?
How dare you keep customers waiting like this?!
But Mama, Ah finished--
I told you to return quickly as we've been so busy lately.
But Mama, you never said--
It doesn't matter what I say, you never listen. I should really--
Please spare me your theatrics. She had no way of knowing I would pay you to stay open as long as need be...

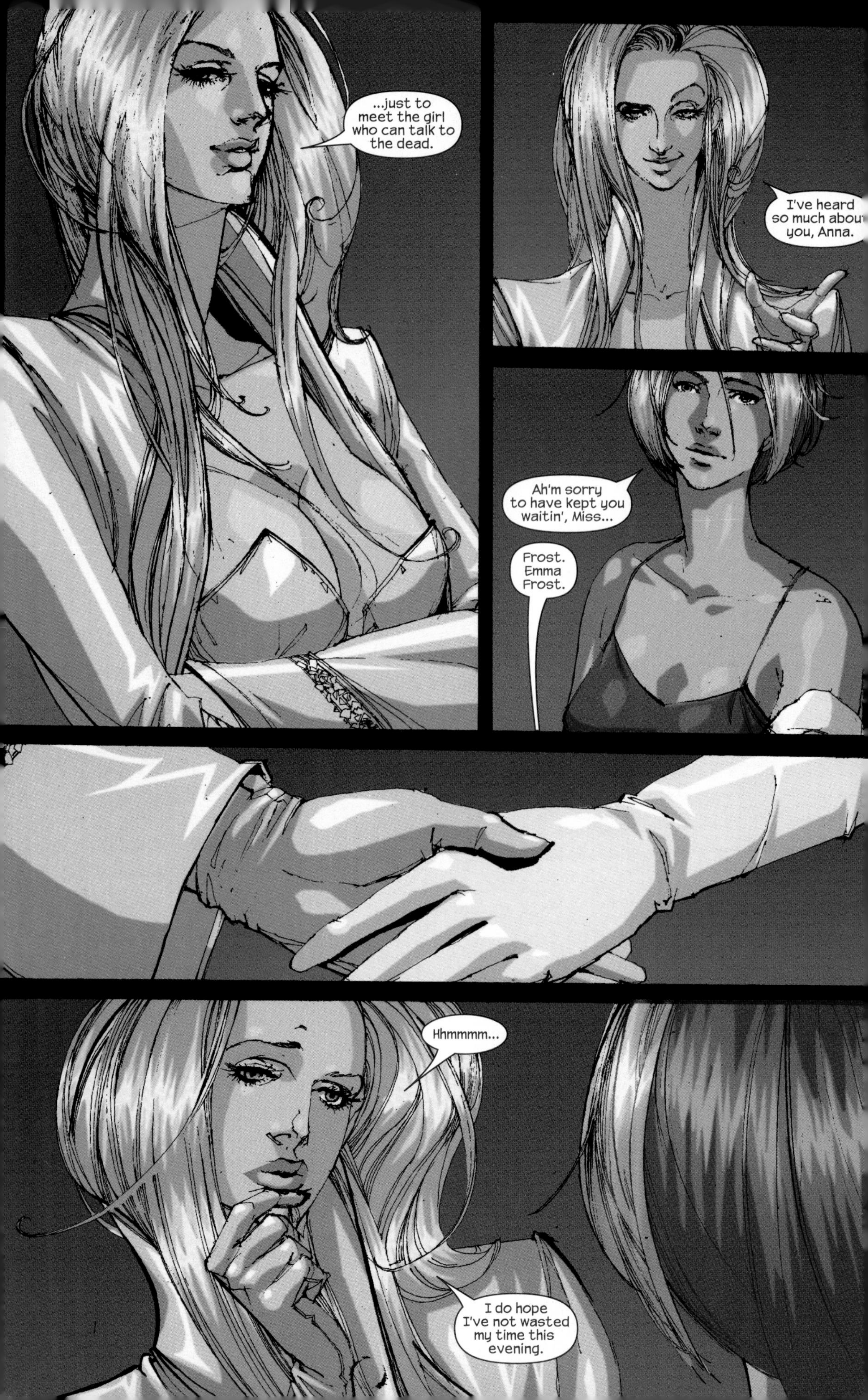
...just to meet the girl who can talk to the dead.
I've heard so much about you, Anna.
Ah'm sorry to have kept you waitin', Miss...
Frost. Emma Frost.
Hhmmmm...
I do hope I've not wasted my time this evening.

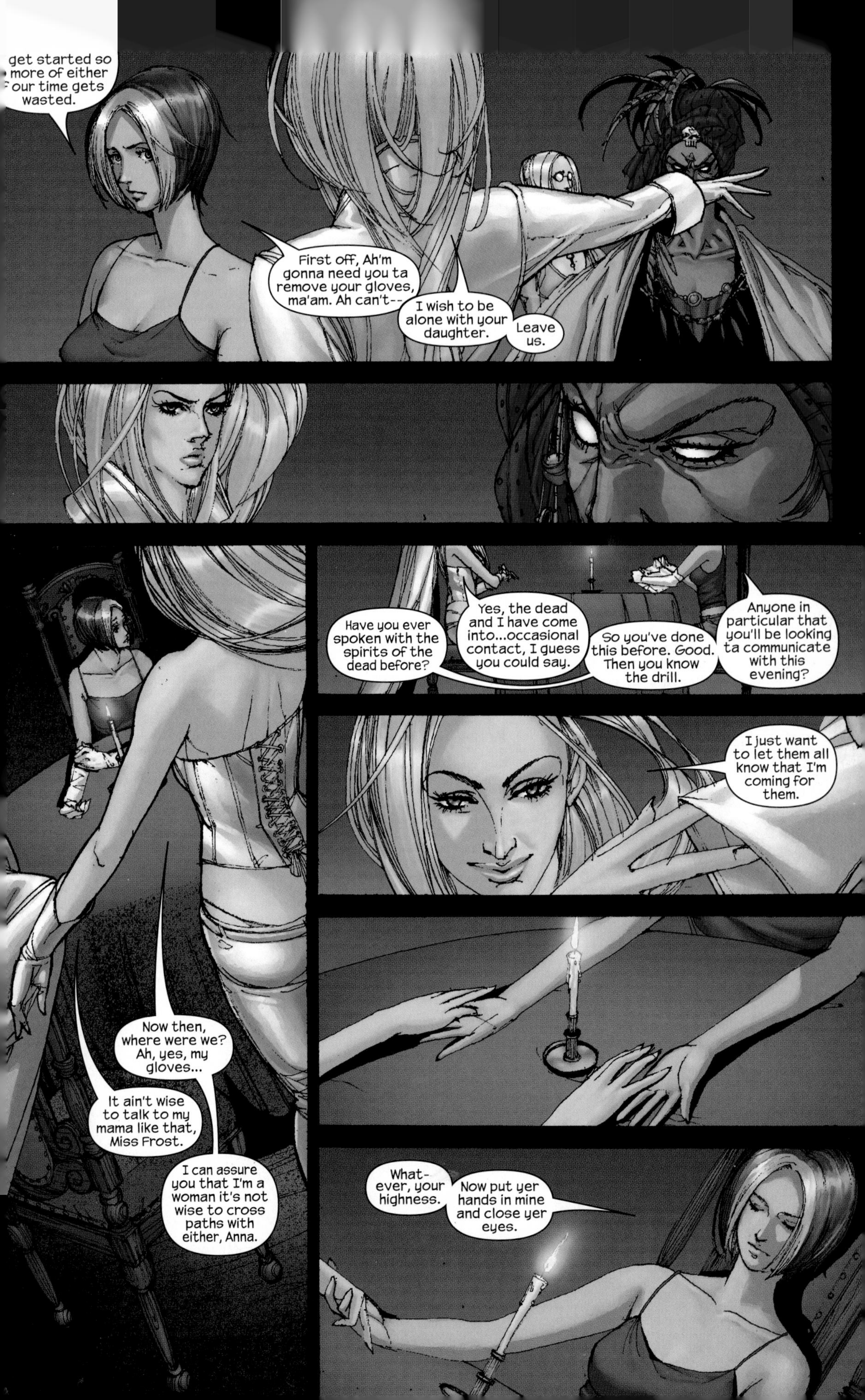
get started so
more of either
our time gets
wasted.
First off, Ah'm gonna need you ta remove your gloves, ma'am. Ah can't--
I wish to be alone with your daughter.
Leave us.
Have you ever spoken with the spirits of the dead before?
Yes, the dead and I have come into...occasional contact, I guess you could say.
So you've done this before. Good. Then you know the drill.
Anyone in particular that you'll be looking ta communicate with this evening?
I just want to let them all know that I'm coming for them.
Now then, where were we? Ah, yes, my gloves...
It ain't wise to talk to my mama like that, Miss Frost.
I can assure you that I'm a woman it's not wise to cross paths with either, Anna.
What-ever, your highness.
Now put yer hands in mine and close yer eyes.

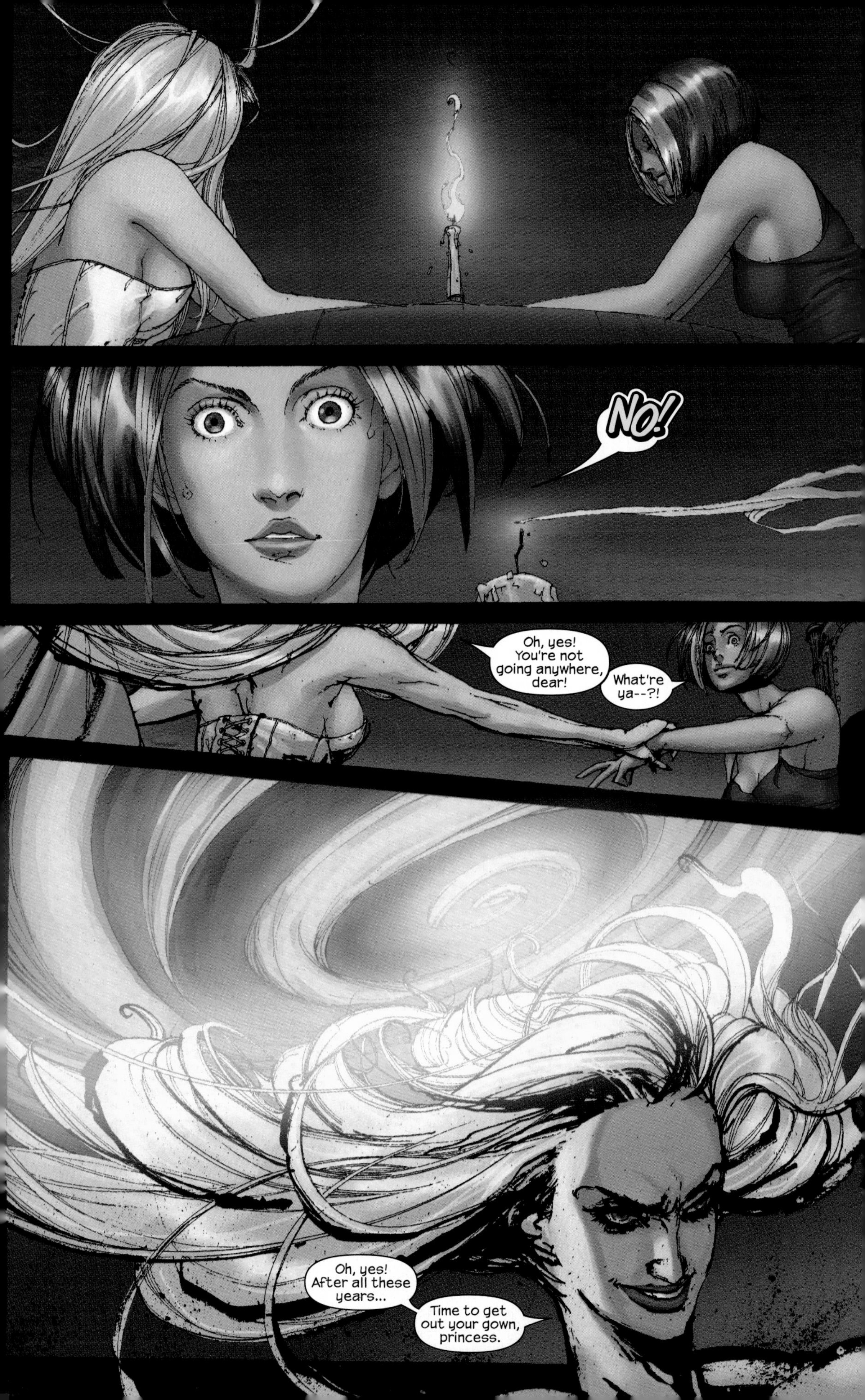
NO!
Oh, yes! You're not going anywhere, dear!
What're ya--?!
Oh, yes! After all these years...
Time to get out your gown, princess.

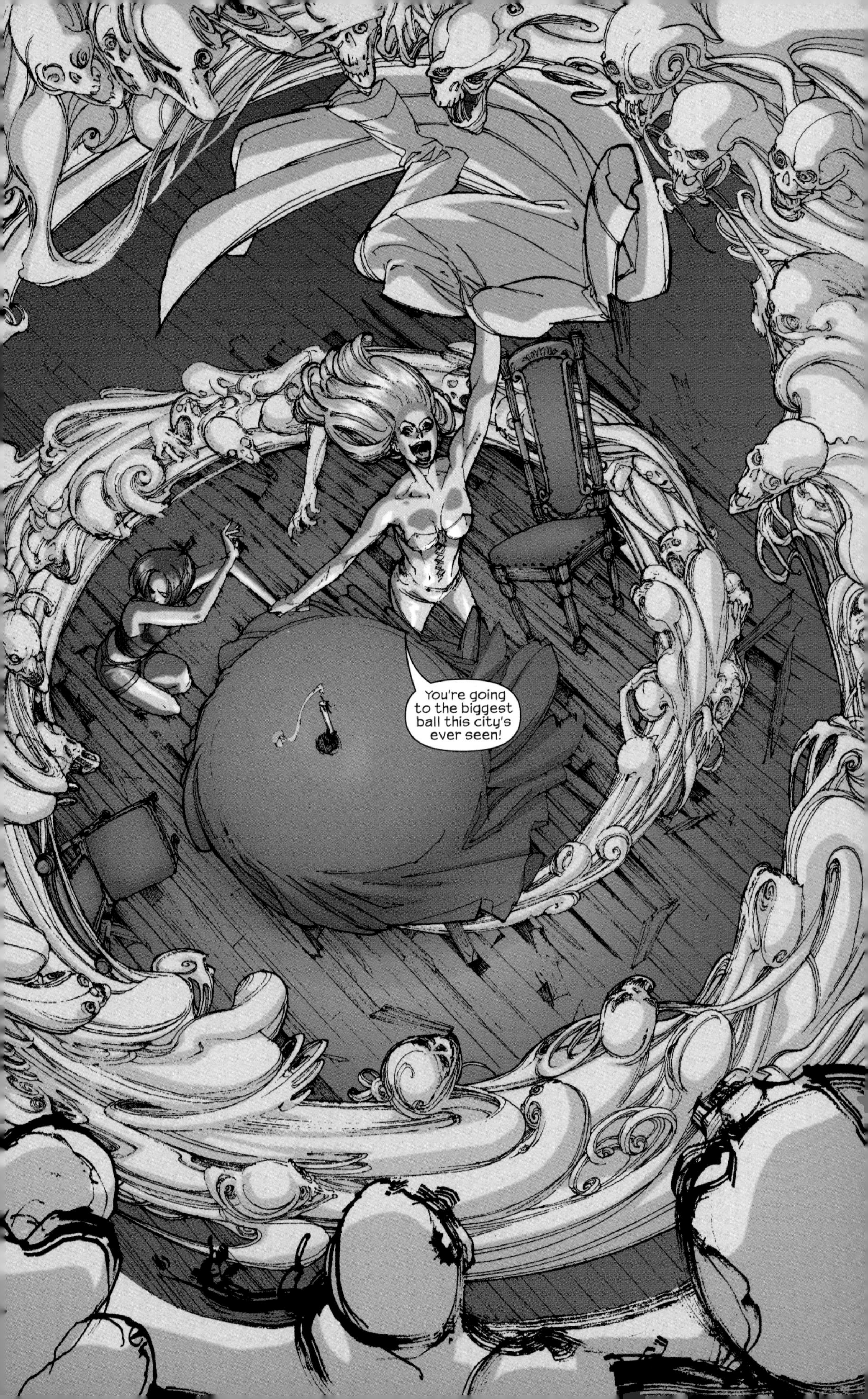
You're going to the biggest ball this city's ever seen!

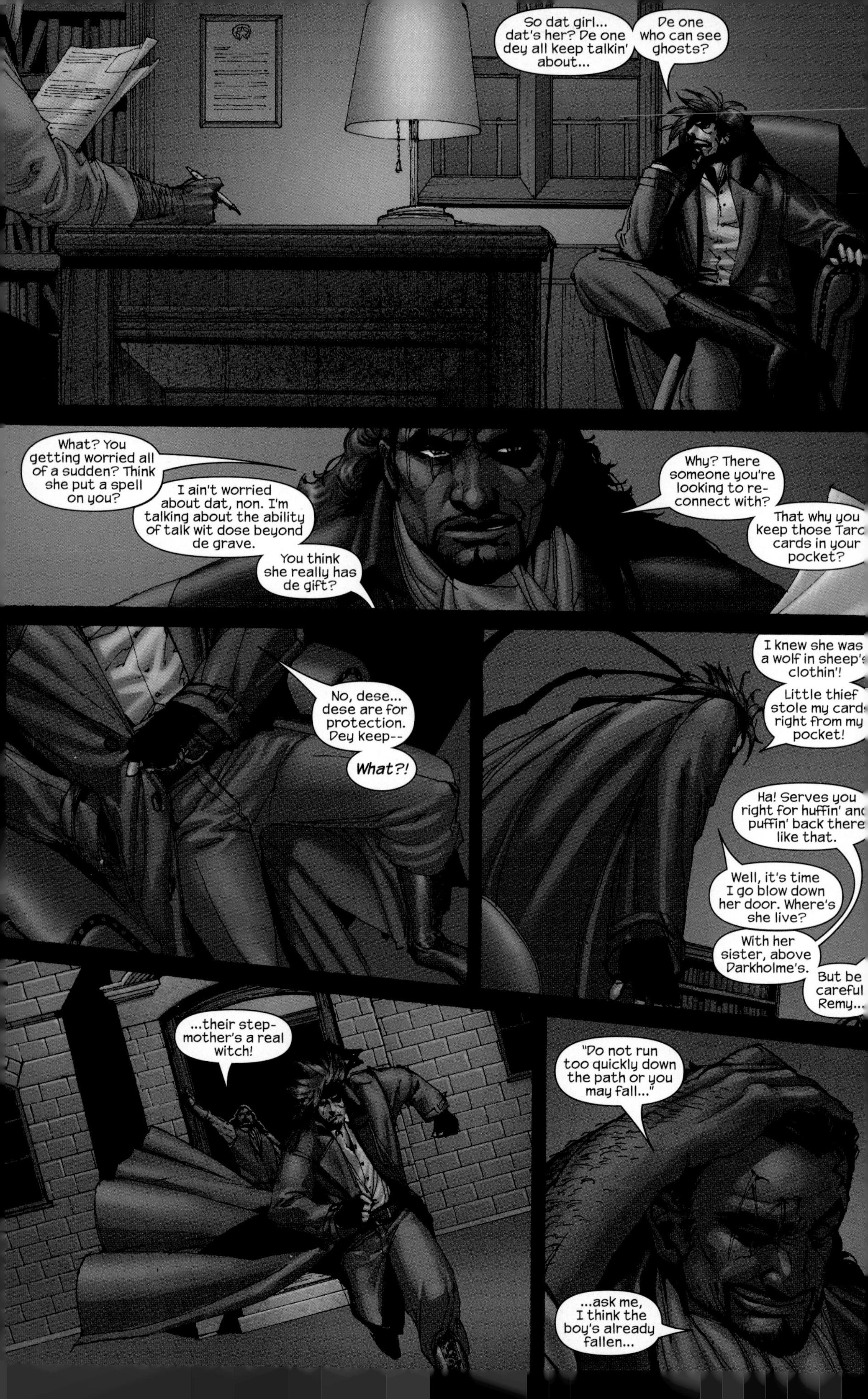
So dat girl... dat's her? De one dey all keep talkin' about...
De one who can see ghosts?
What? You getting worried all of a sudden? Think she put a spell on you?
I ain't worried about dat, non. I'm talking about the ability of talk wit dose beyond de grave.
You think she really has de gift?
Why? There someone you're looking to re-connect with?
That why you keep those Tarc cards in your pocket?
No, dese... dese are for protection. Dey keep--
What?!
I knew she was a wolf in sheep's clothin'!
Little thief stole my card right from my pocket!
Ha! Serves you right for huffin' anc puffin' back there like that.
Well, it's time I go blow down her door. Where's she live?
With her sister, above Darkholme's.
But be careful Remy...
...their step-mother's a real witch!
"Do not run too quickly down the path or you may fall..."
...ask me, I think the boy's already fallen...

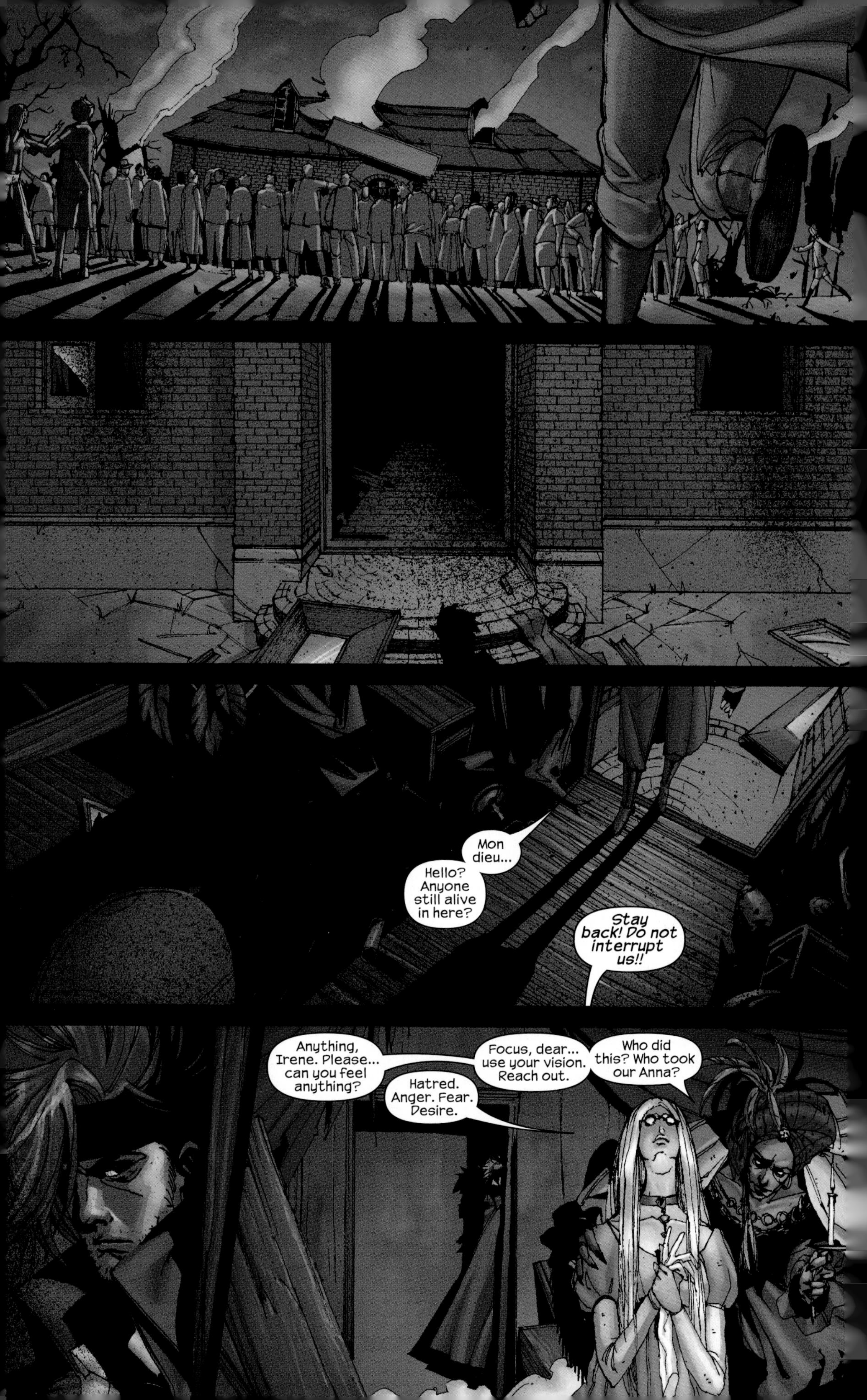

Mon dieu...
Hello? Anyone still alive in here?
Stay back! Do not interrupt us!!
Anything, Irene. Please... can you feel anything?
Hatred. Anger. Fear. Desire.
Focus, dear... use your vision. Reach out.
Who did this? Who took our Anna?

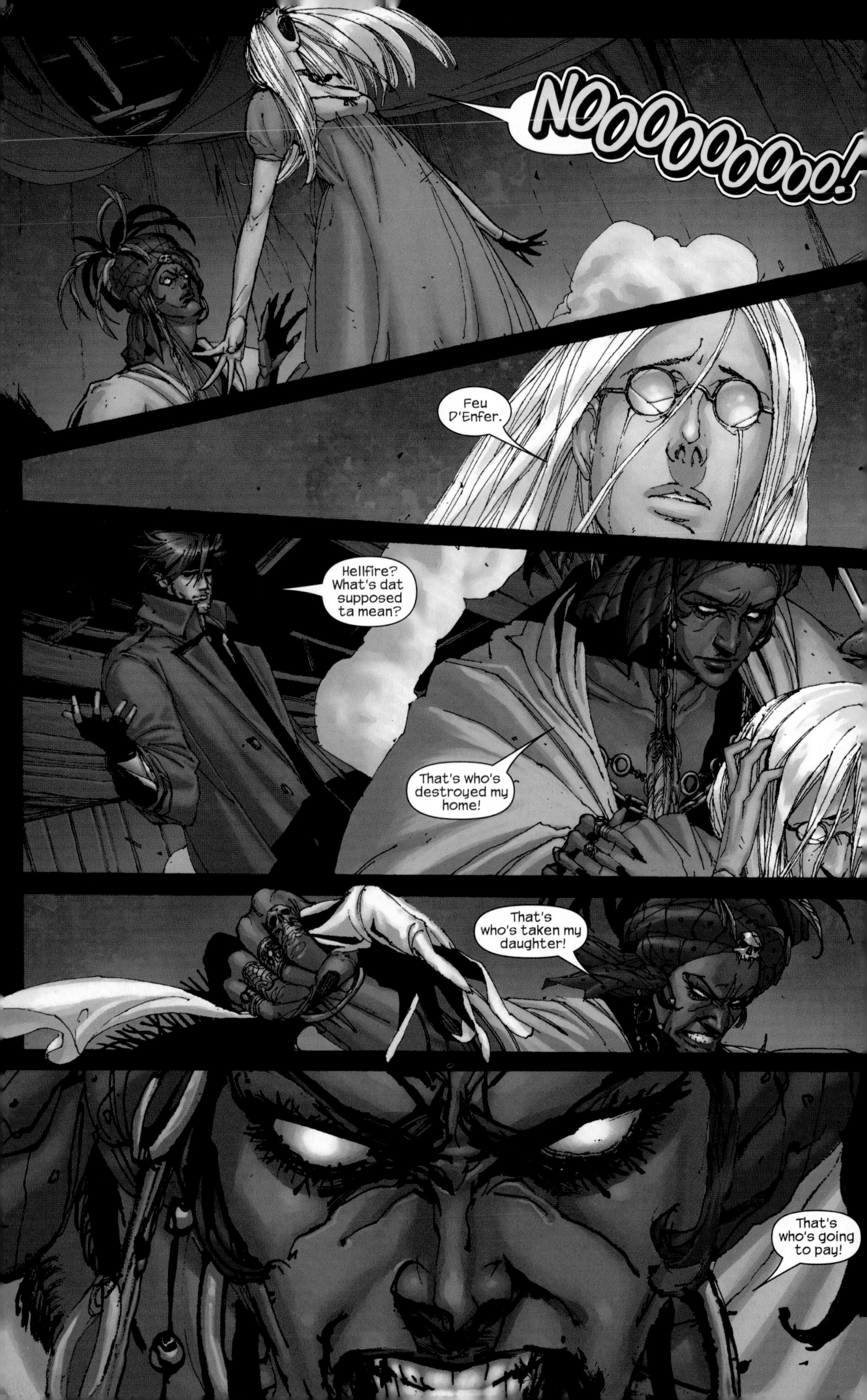
NOOOOOOOOOO!
Feu D'Enfer.
Hellfire? What's dat supposed ta mean?
That's who's destroyed my home!
That's who's taken my daughter!
That's who's going to pay!

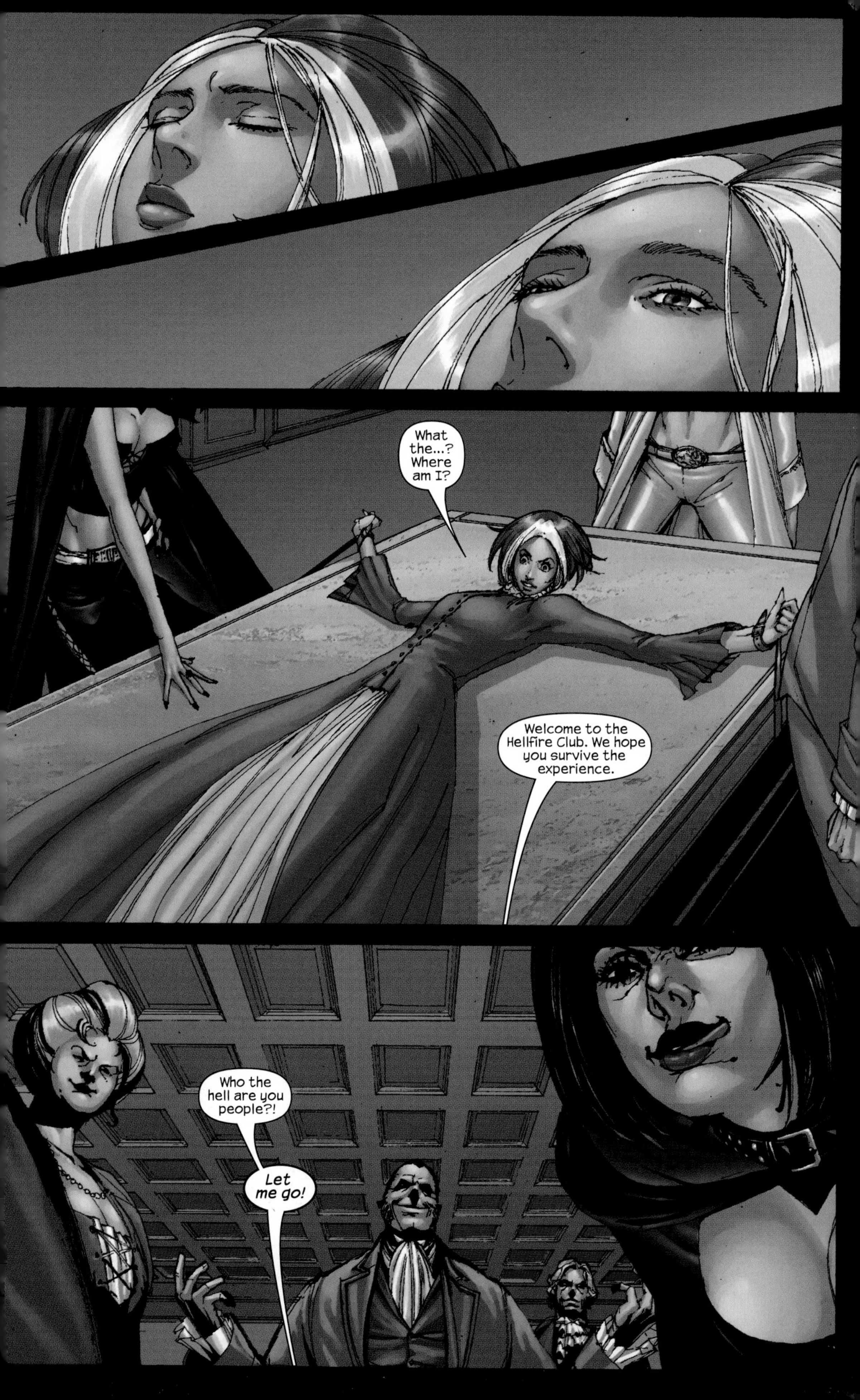
What the...? Where am I?
Welcome to the Hellfire Club. We hope you survive the experience.
Who the hell are you people?!
Let me go!

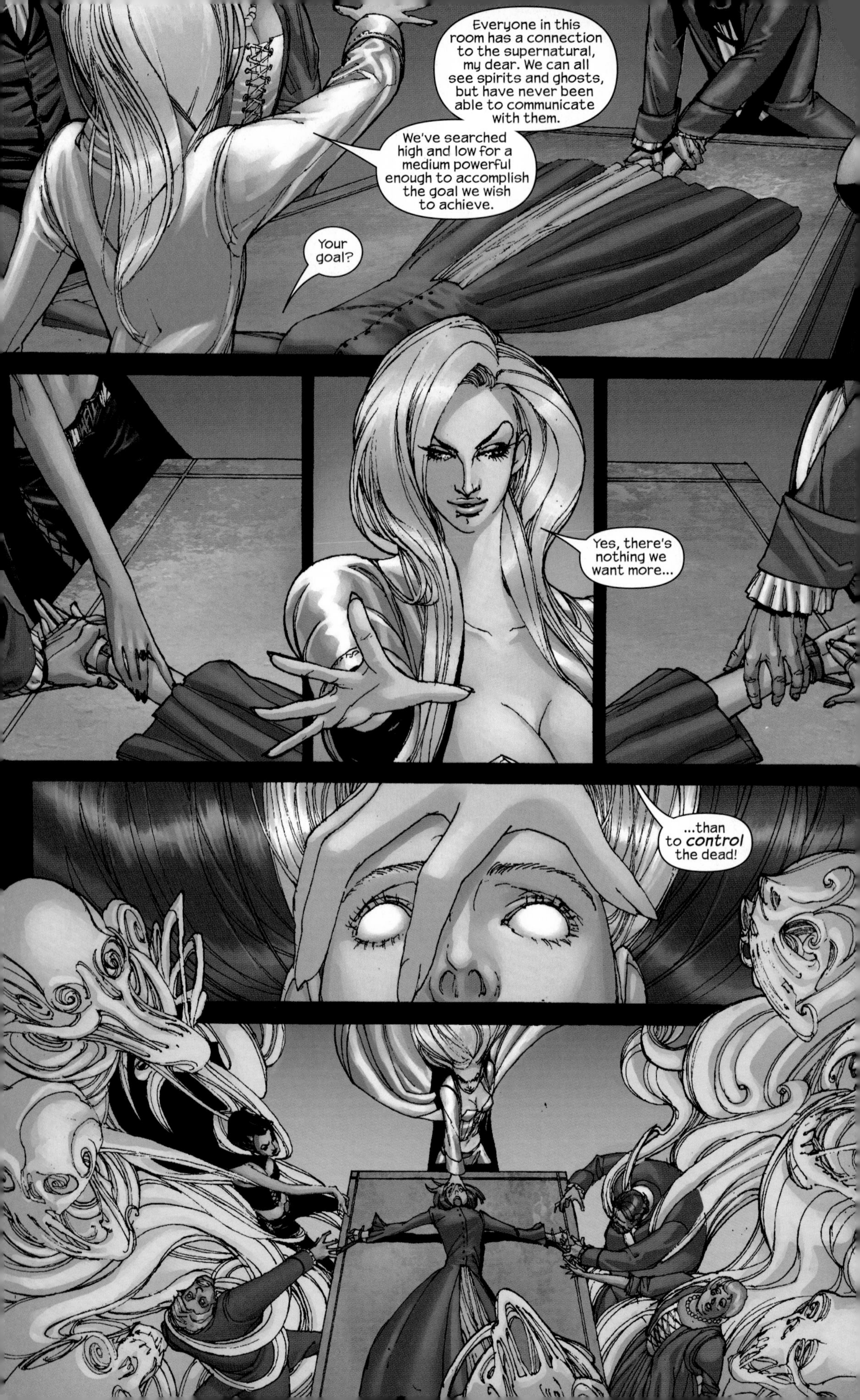
Everyone in this room has a connection to the supernatural, my dear. We can all see spirits and ghosts, but have never been able to communicate with them.
We've searched high and low for a medium powerful enough to accomplish the goal we wish to achieve.
Your goal?
Yes, there's nothing we want more...
...than to *control* the dead!

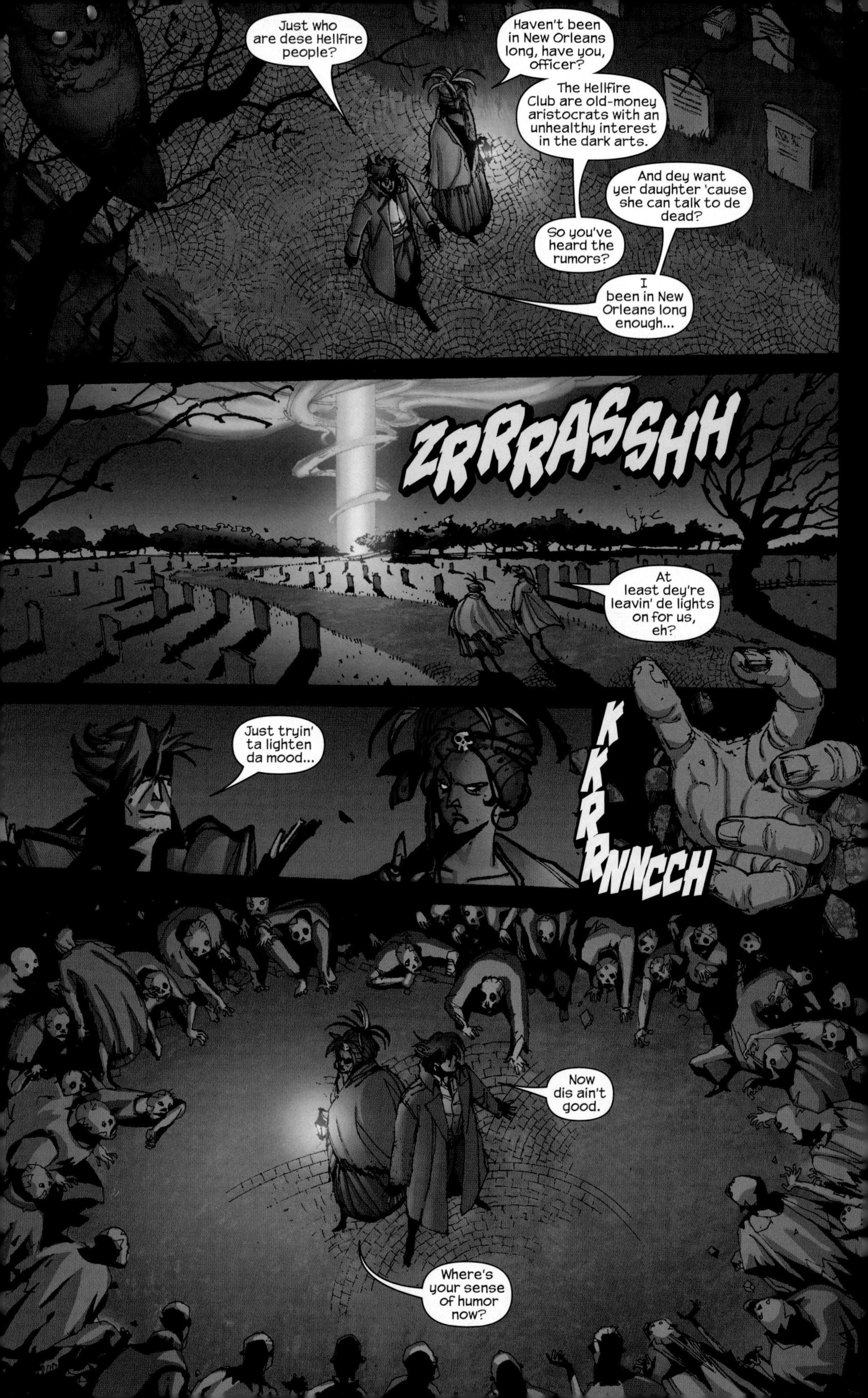
Just who are dese Hellfire people?
Haven't been in New Orleans long, have you, officer?
The Hellfire Club are old-money aristocrats with an unhealthy interest in the dark arts.
So you've heard the rumors?
And dey want yer daughter 'cause she can talk to de dead?
I been in New Orleans long enough...
ZRRRASSHH
At least dey're leavin' de lights on for us, eh?
Just tryin' ta lighten da mood...
KKRRNNCCH
Now dis ain't good.
Where's your sense of humor now?

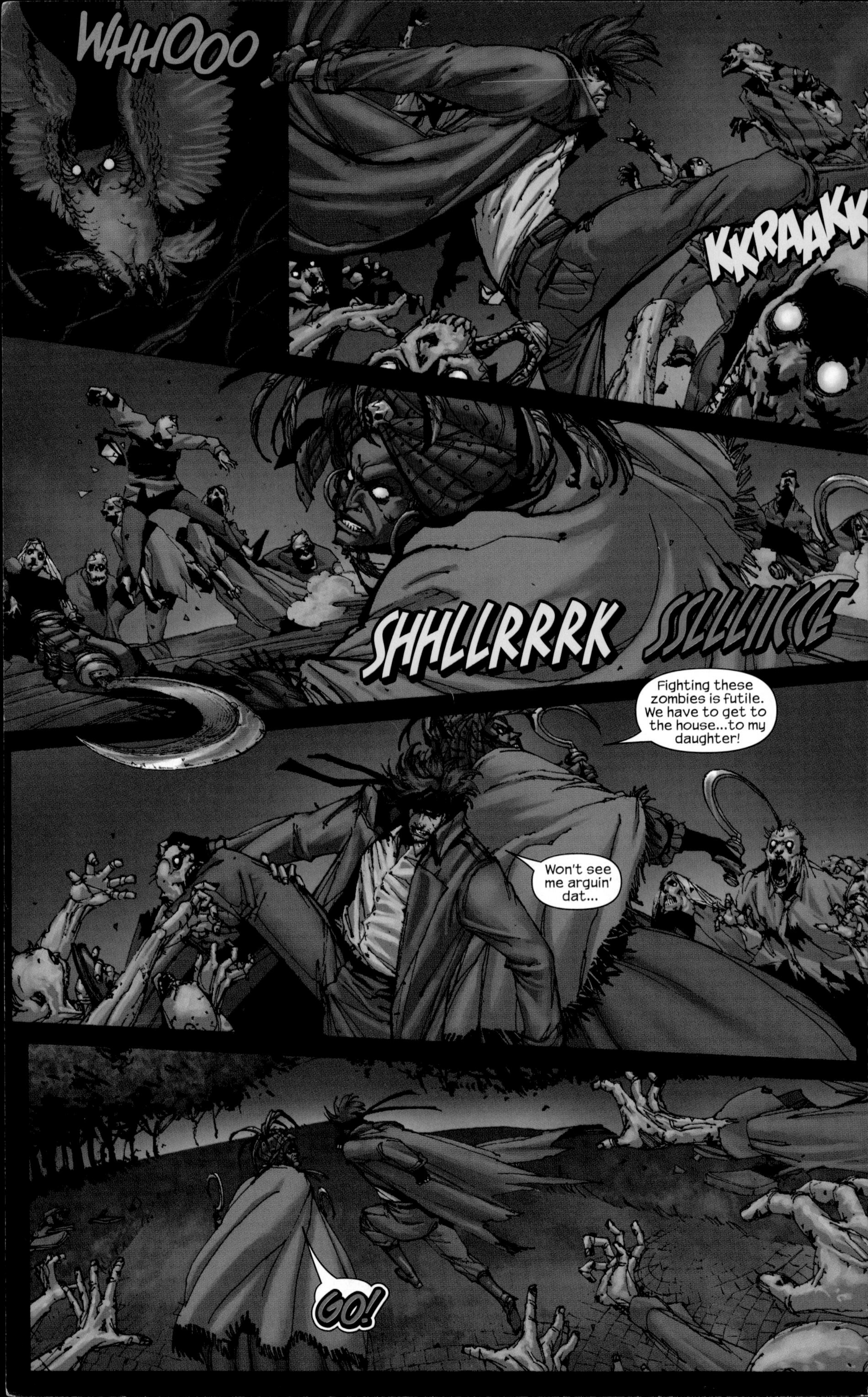
WHHOOO
KKRAAKK
SHHLLRRRK
SSLLLICE
Fighting these zombies is futile. We have to get to the house...to my daughter!
Won't see me arguin' dat...
GO!

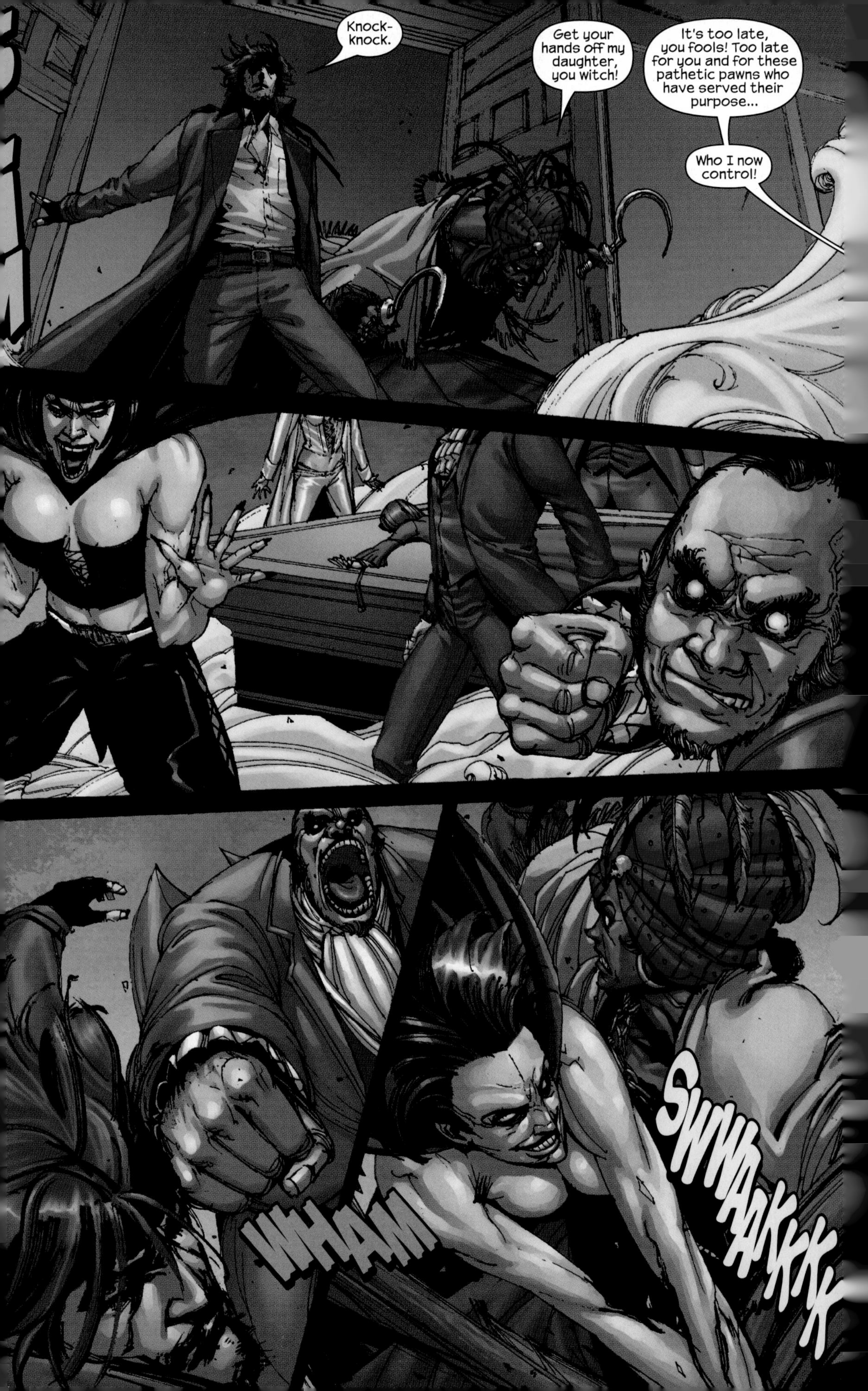

Knock-knock.
Get your hands off my daughter, you witch!
It's too late, you fools! Too late for you and for these pathetic pawns who have served their purpose...
Who I now control!
WHAM
SWWAAKKKK

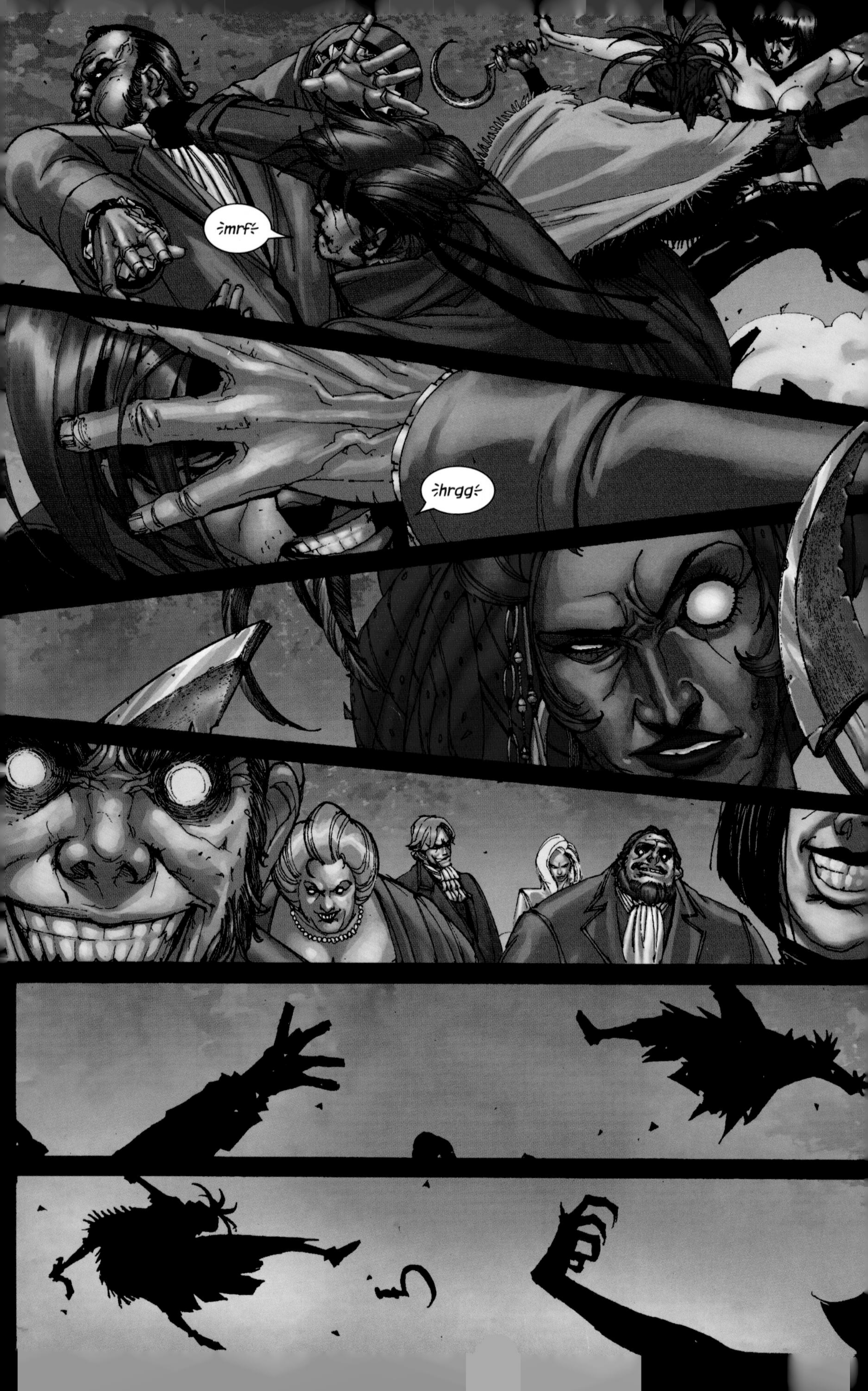
mrf
hrgg

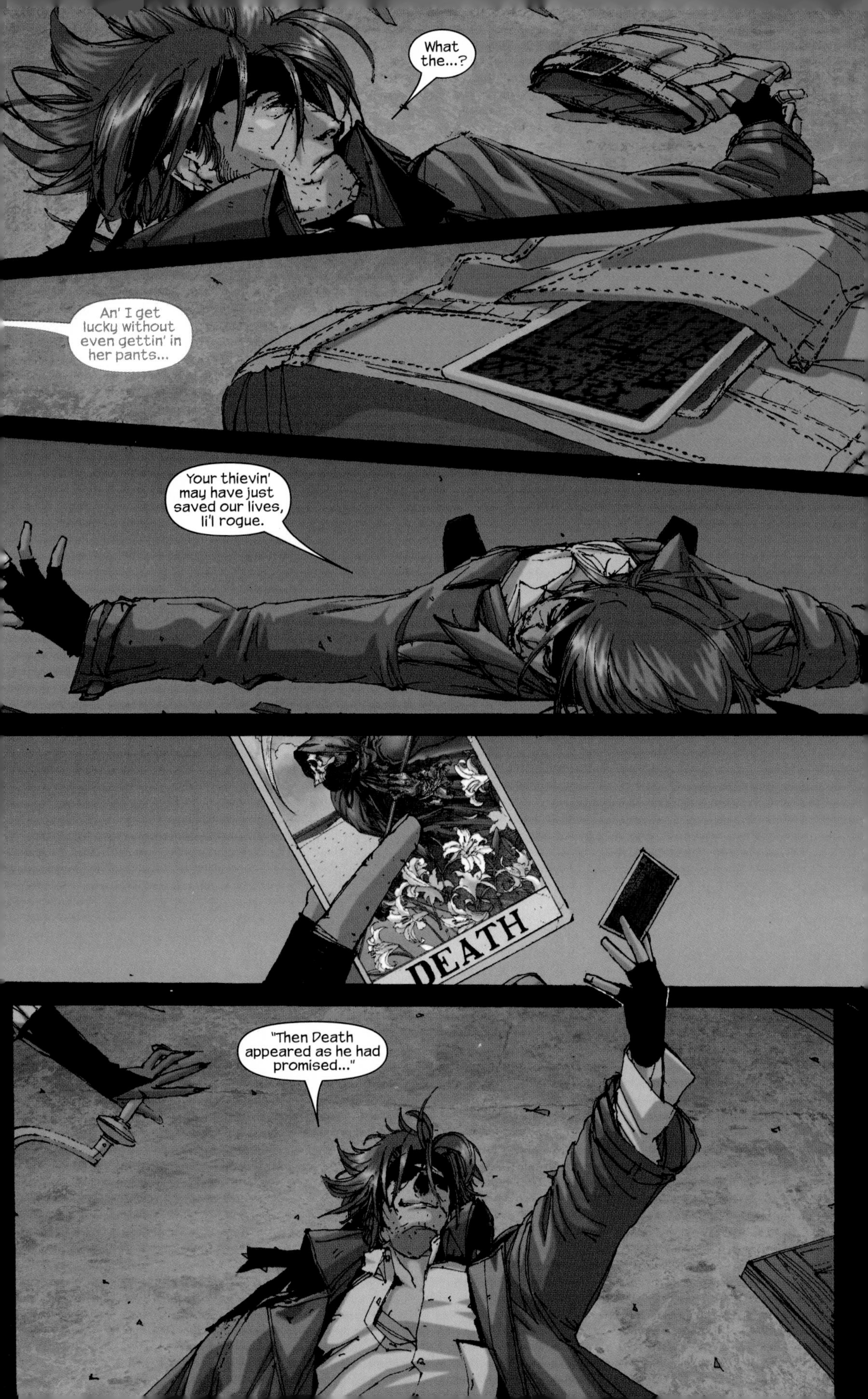
What the...?
An' I get lucky without even gettin' in her pants...
Your thievin' may have just saved our lives, li'l rogue.
DEATH
"Then Death appeared as he had promised..."

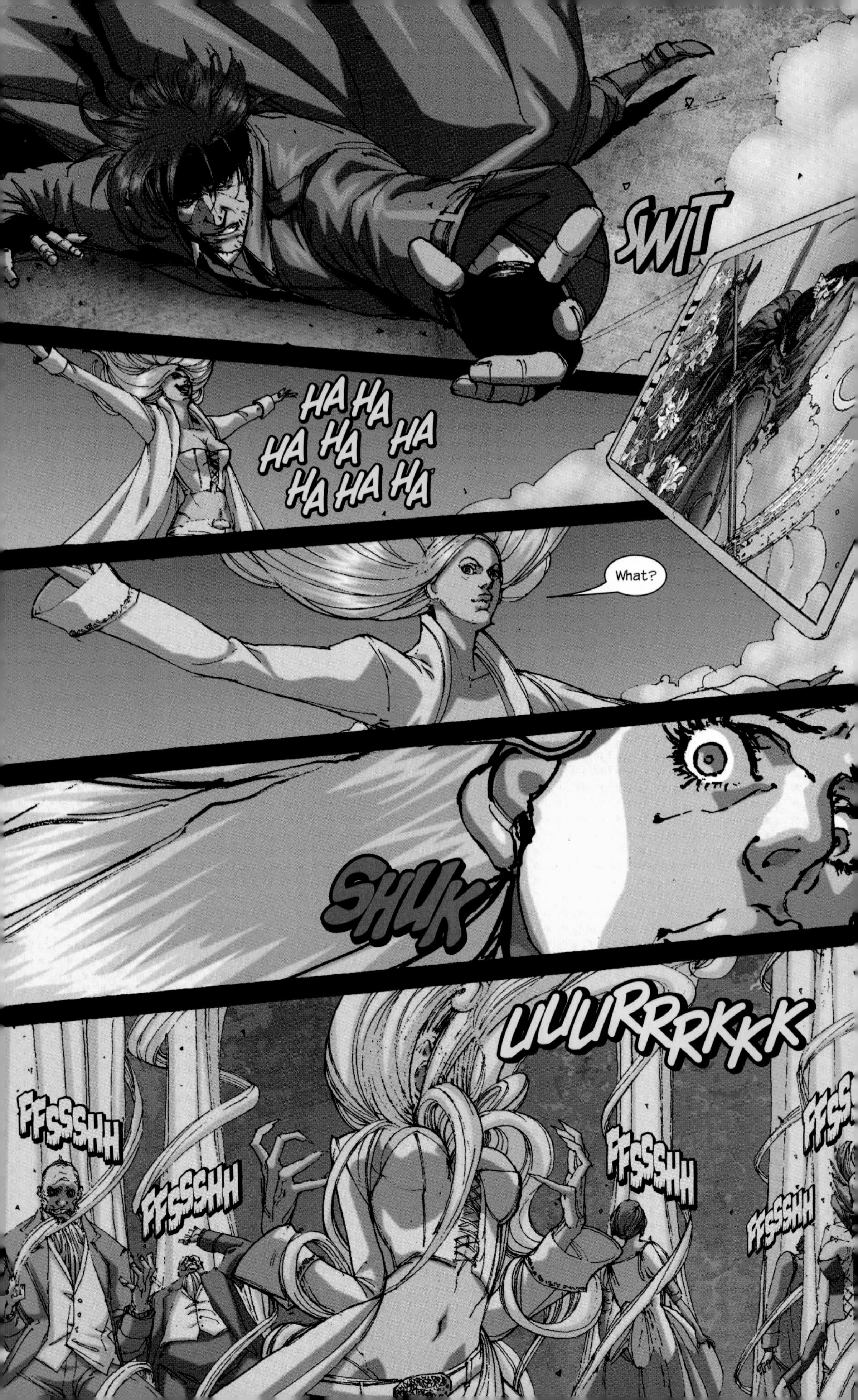
SWIT
HA HA
HA HA HA
HA HA HA
What?
SHUK
UUURRRKKK
FFSSSHH
FFSSSHH
FFSSSHH
FFSSSHH

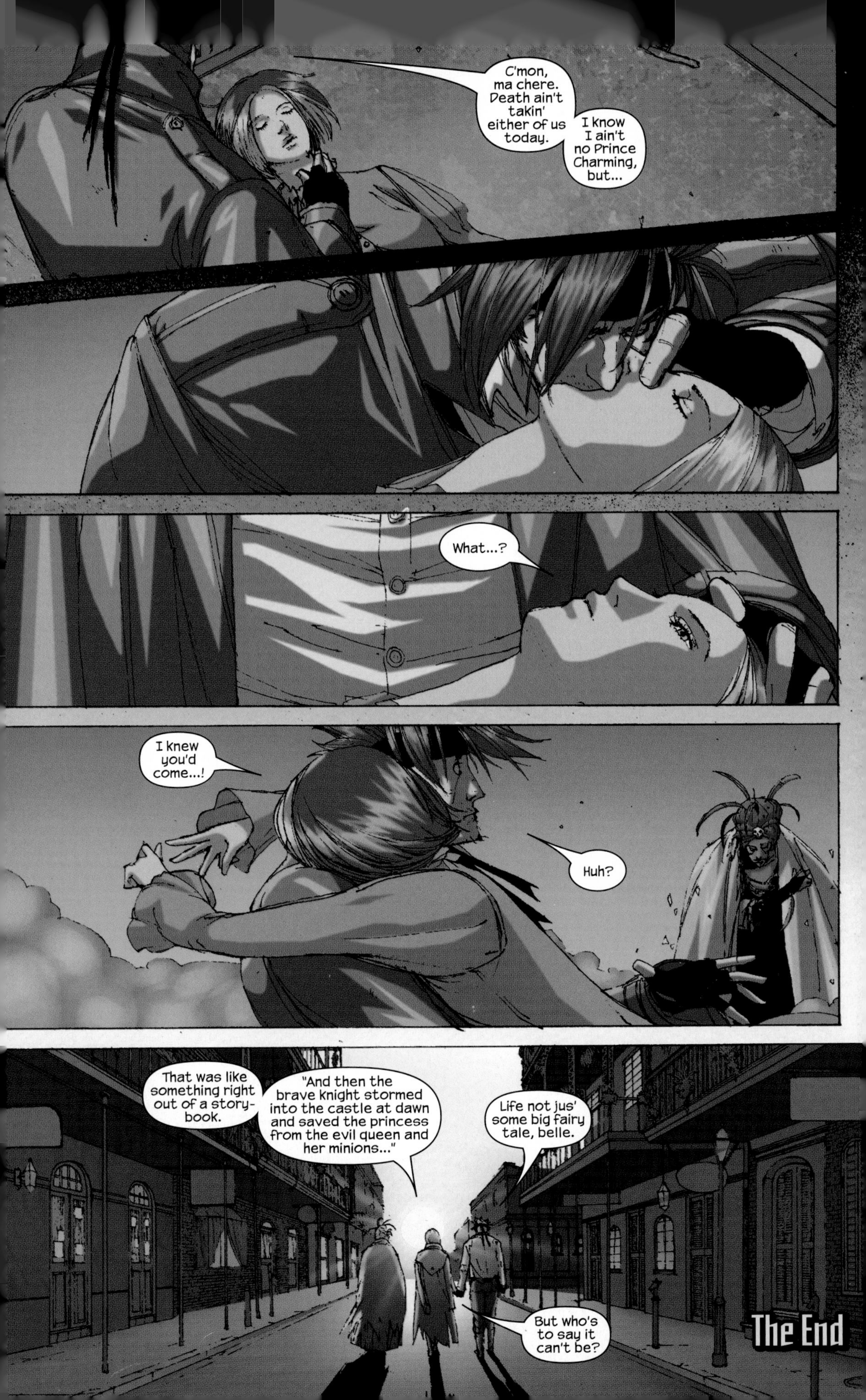
C'mon, ma chere. Death ain't takin' either of us today.
I know I ain't no Prince Charming, but...
What...?
I knew you'd come...!
Huh?
That was like something right out of a story-book.
"And then the brave knight stormed into the castle at dawn and saved the princess from the evil queen and her minions..."
Life not jus' some big fairy tale, belle.
But who's to say it can't be?
The End

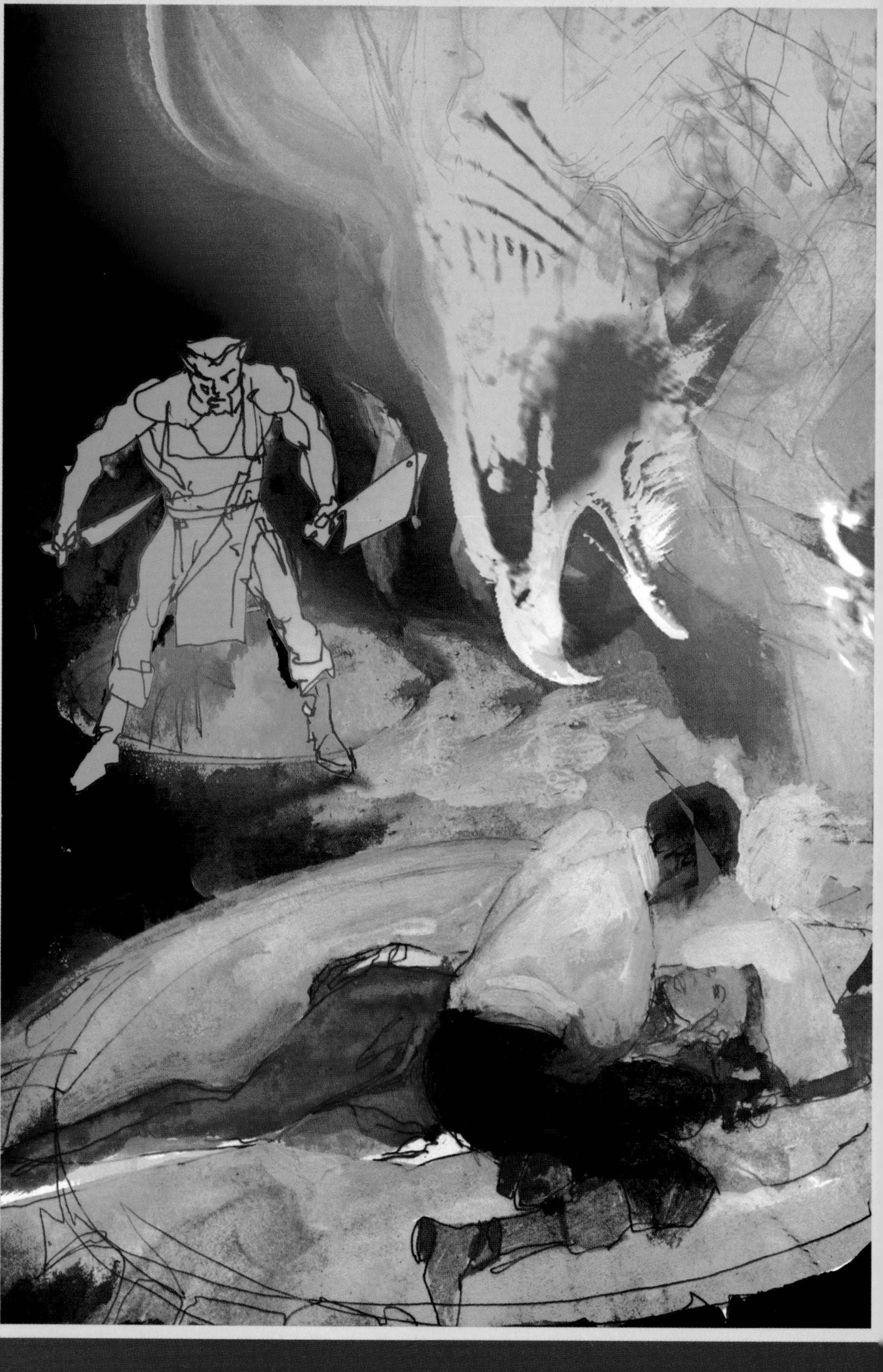

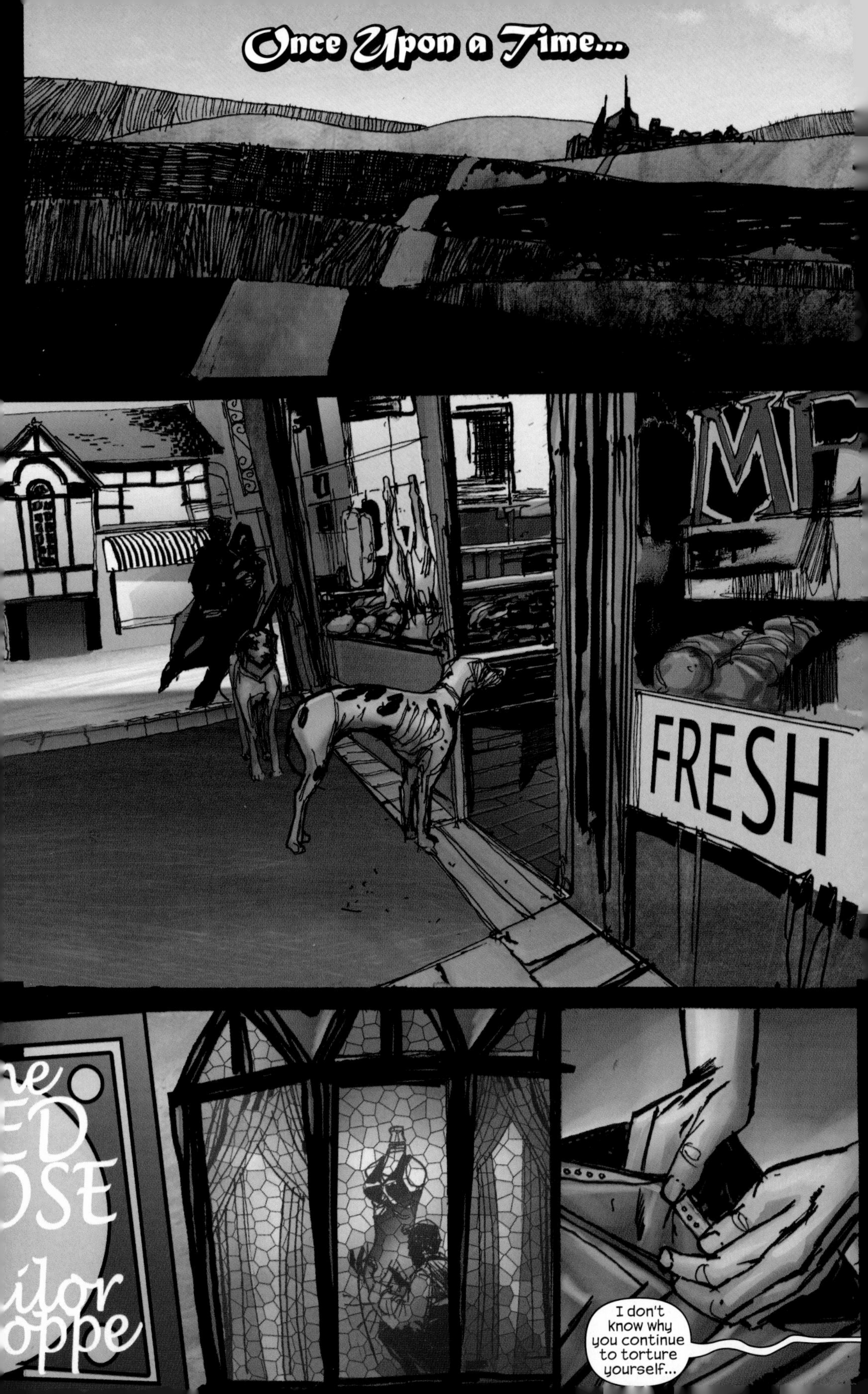
Once Upon a Time...
FRESH
I don't know why you continue to torture yourself...

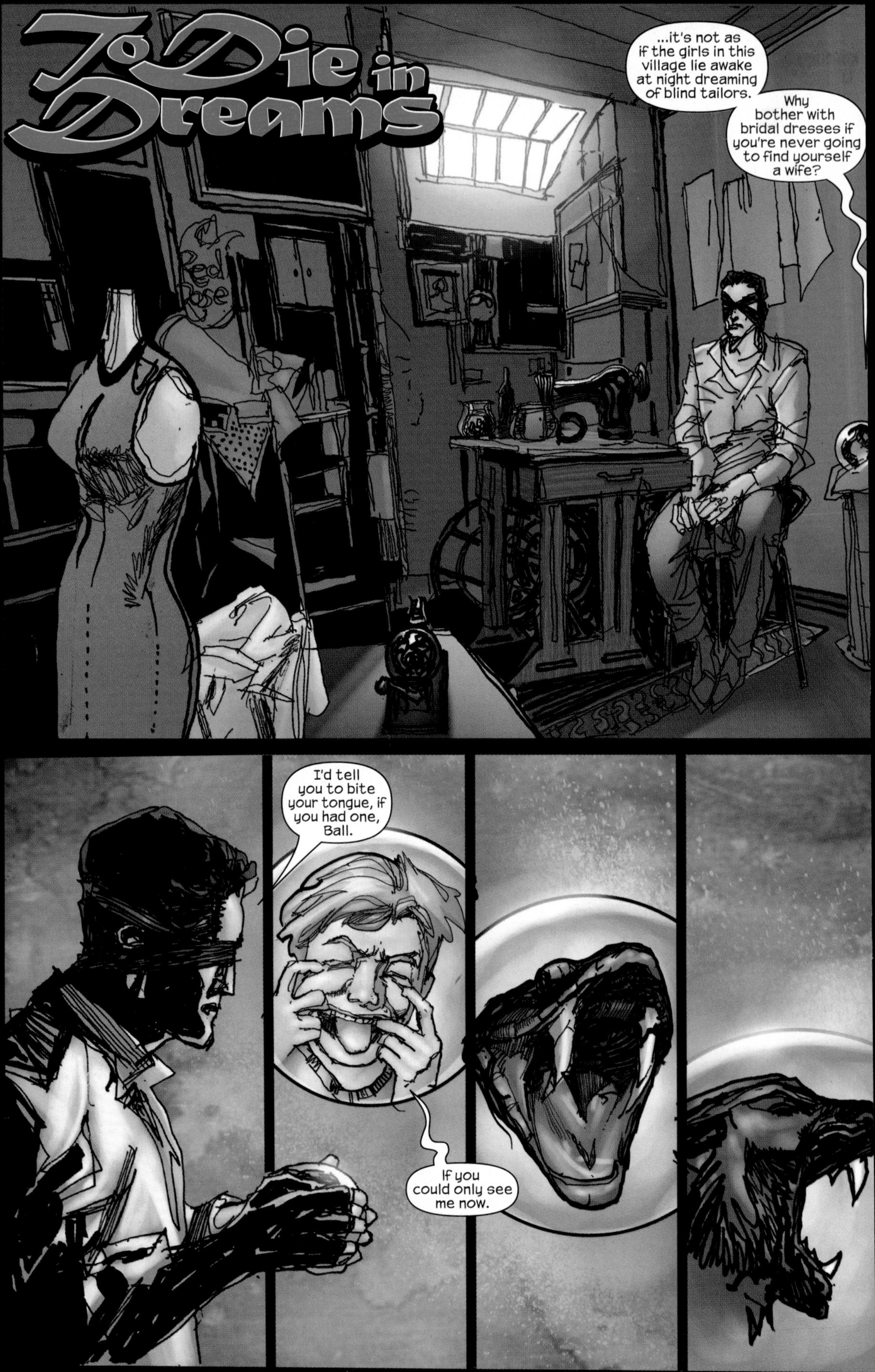
To Die in Dreams
...it's not as if the girls in this village lie awake at night dreaming of blind tailors.
Why bother with bridal dresses if you're never going to find yourself a wife?
Red Rose
I'd tell you to bite your tongue, if you had one, Ball.
If you could only see me now.

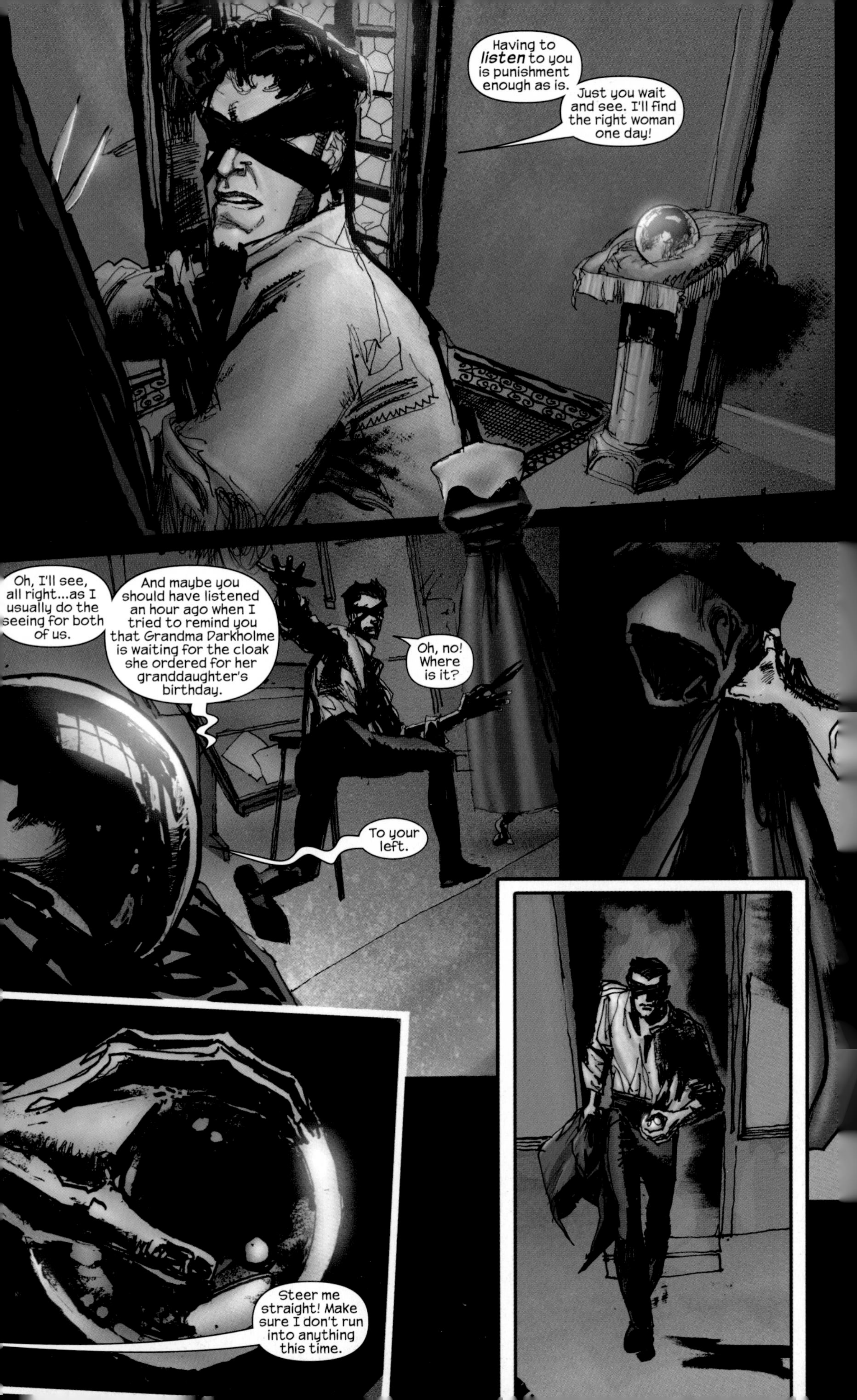

Having to *listen* to you is punishment enough as is.
Just you wait and see. I'll find the right woman one day!
Oh, I'll see, all right...as I usually do the seeing for both of us.
And maybe you should have listened an hour ago when I tried to remind you that Grandma Darkholme is waiting for the cloak she ordered for her granddaughter's birthday.
Oh, no! Where is it?
To your left.
Steer me straight! Make sure I don't run into anything this time.

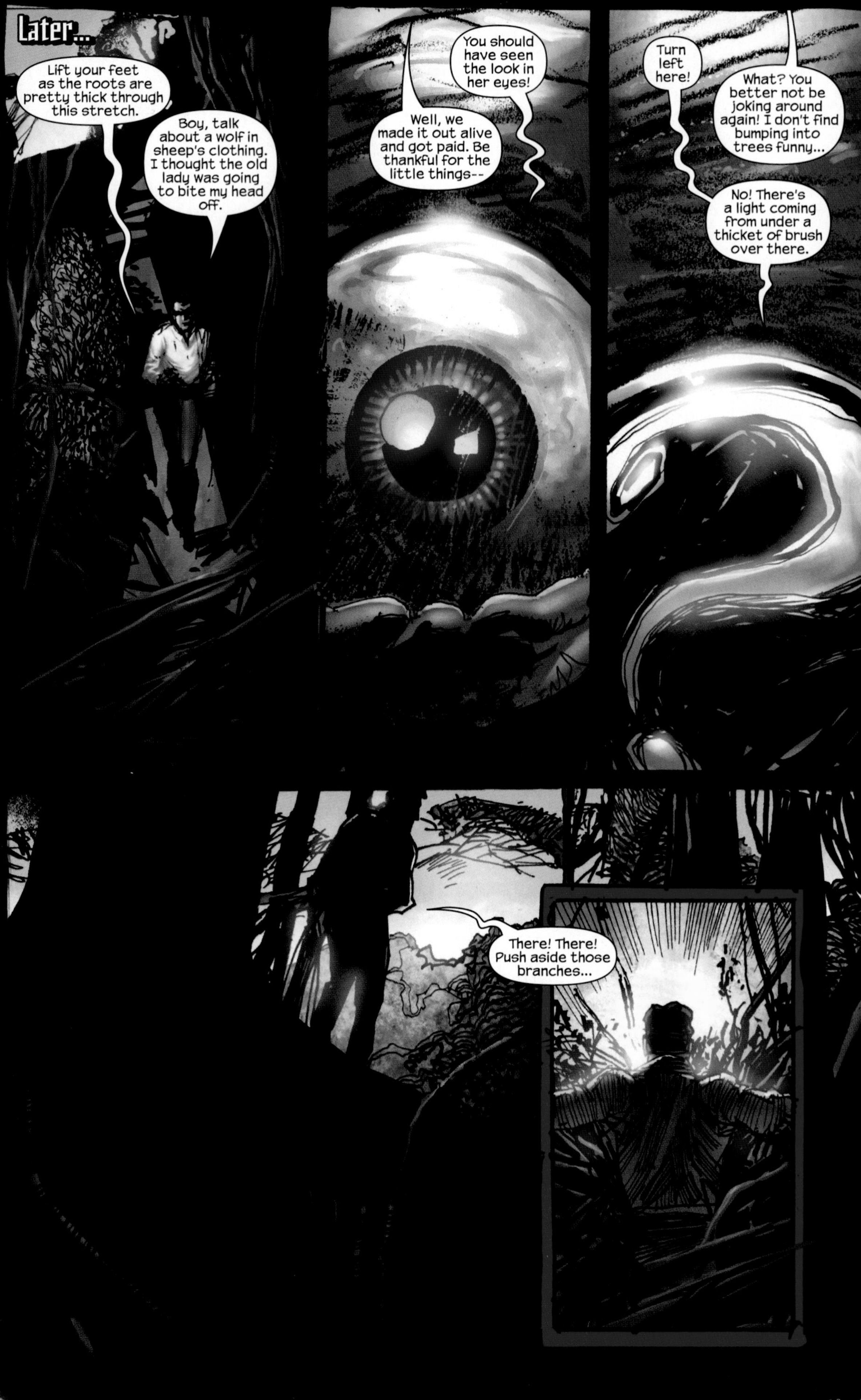
Later...
Lift your feet as the roots are pretty thick through this stretch.
Boy, talk about a wolf in sheep's clothing. I thought the old lady was going to bite my head off.
Well, we made it out alive and got paid. Be thankful for the little things--
You should have seen the look in her eyes!
Turn left here!
What? You better not be joking around again! I don't find bumping into trees funny...
No! There's a light coming from under a thicket of brush over there.
There! There! Push aside those branches...

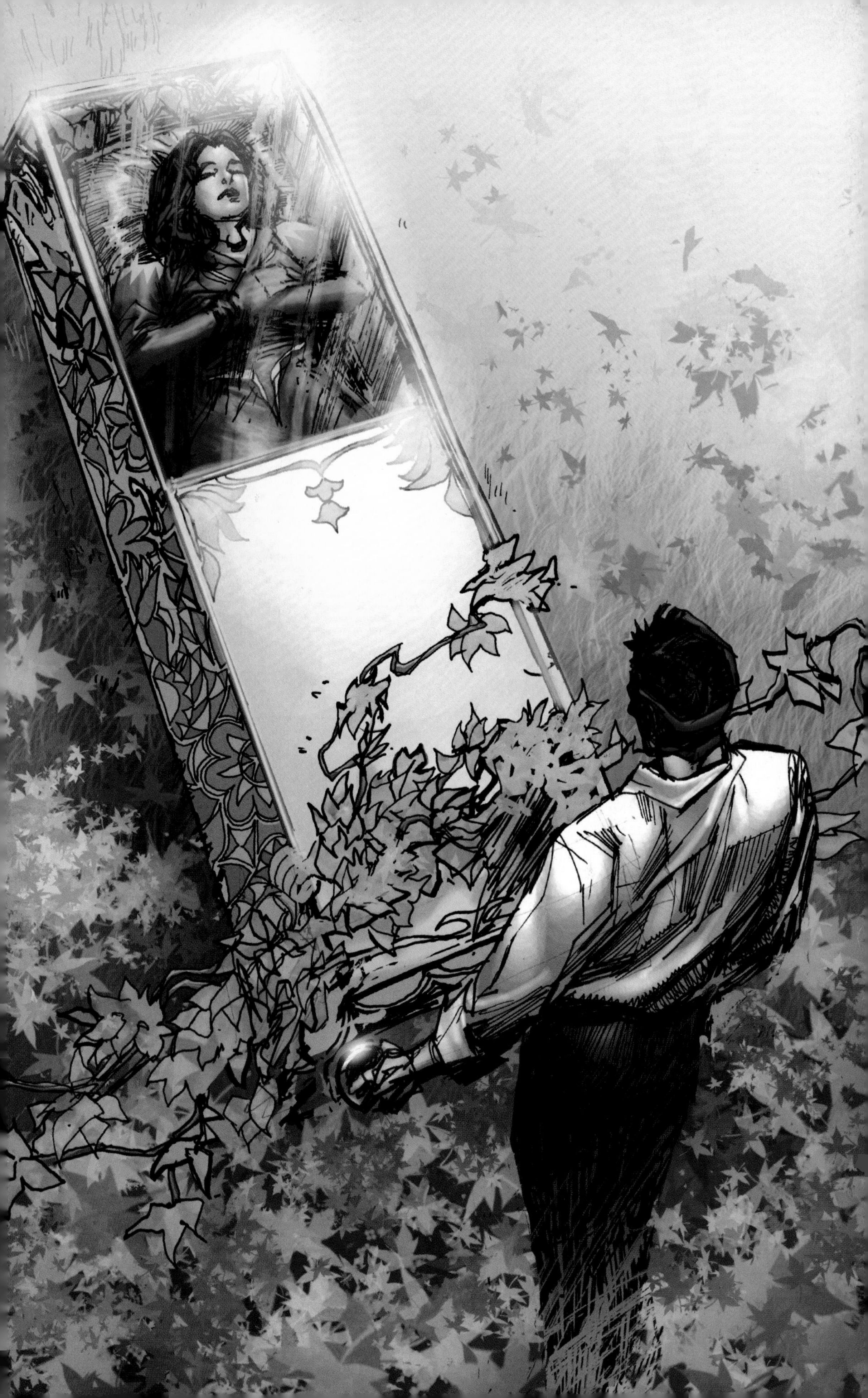

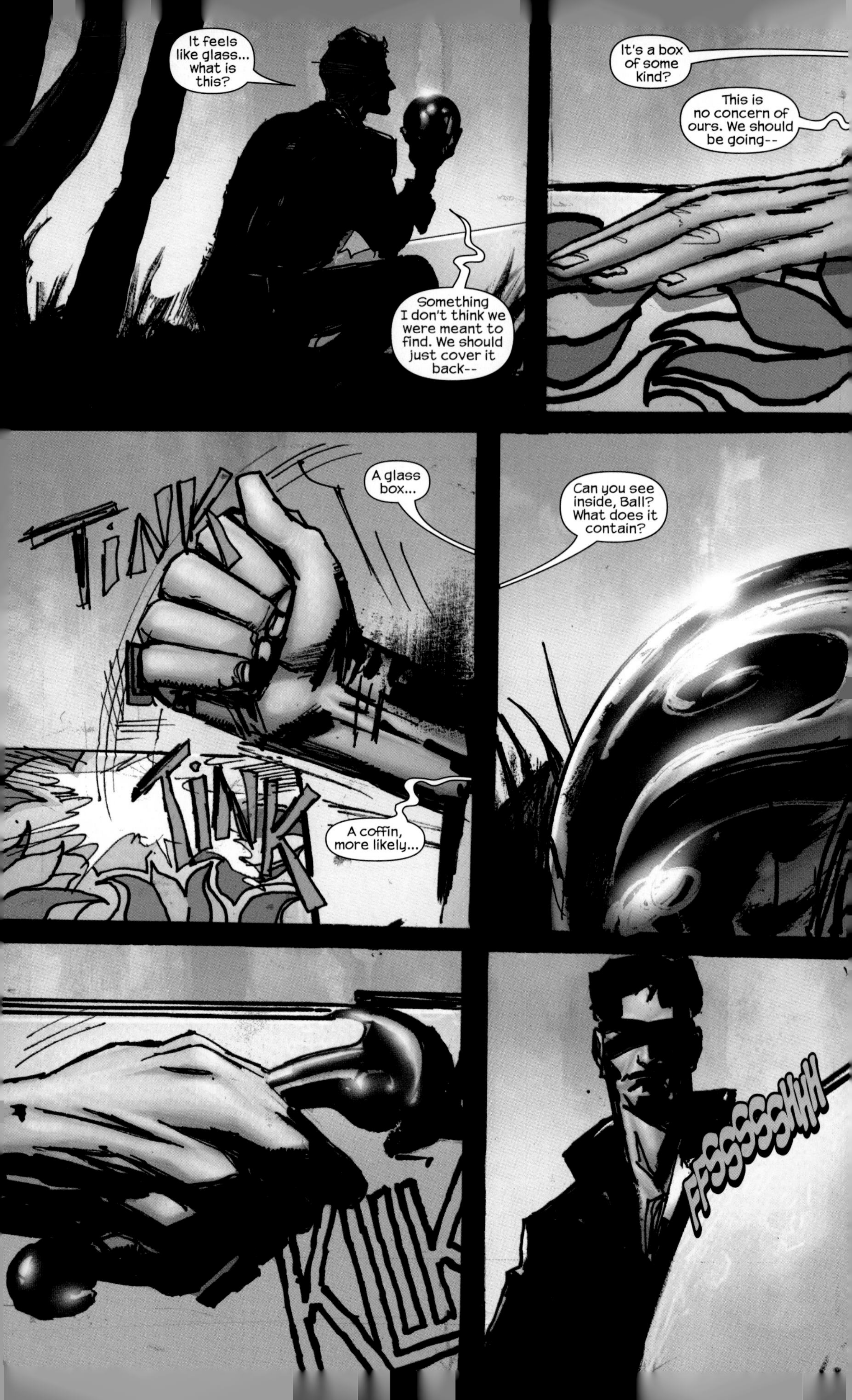
It feels like glass... what is this?
Something I don't think we were meant to find. We should just cover it back--
It's a box of some kind?
This is no concern of ours. We should be going--
TINK
A glass box...
TINK
A coffin, more likely...
Can you see inside, Ball? What does it contain?
KLIK
FFSSSSSHHH

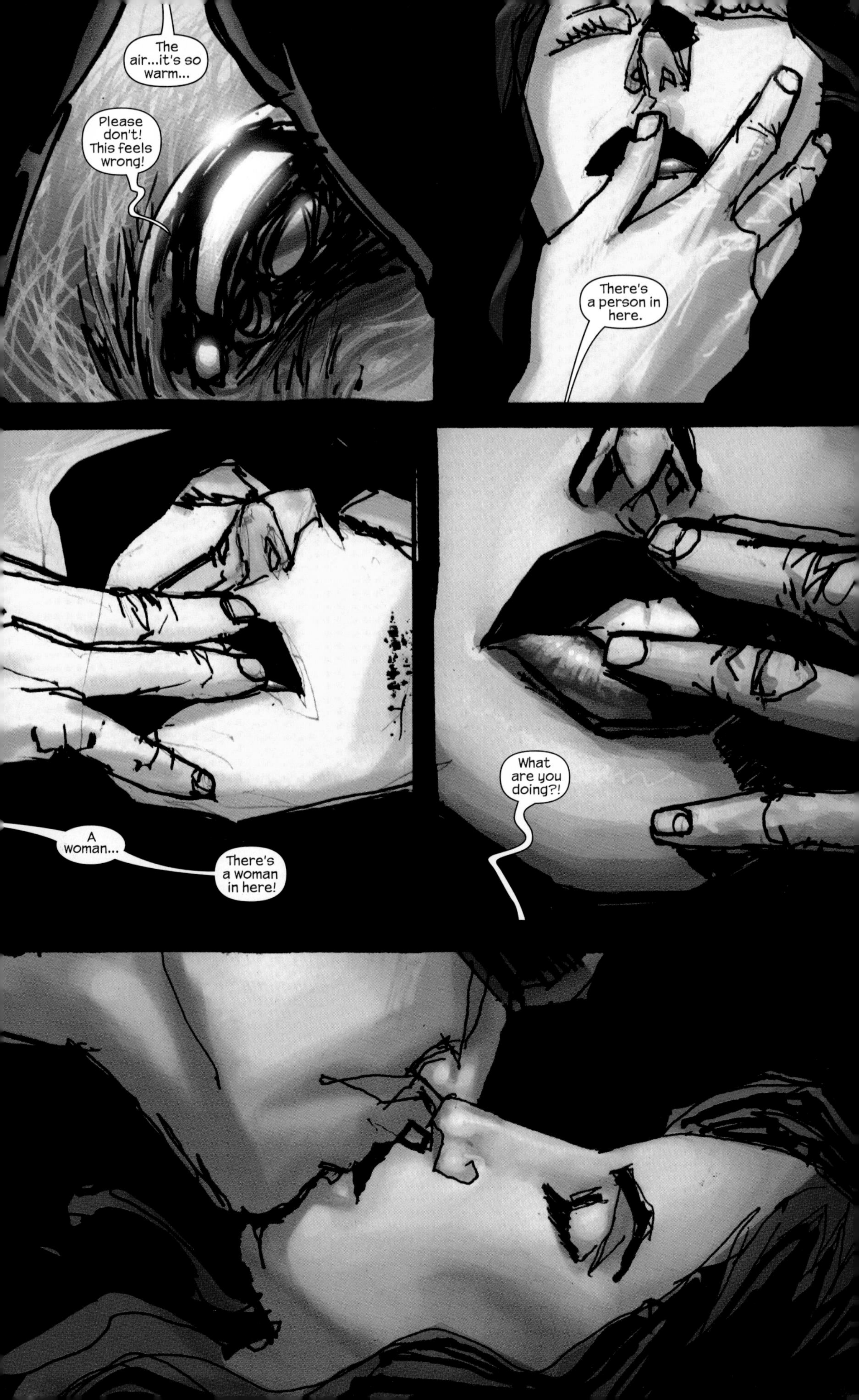
The air...it's so warm...
Please don't! This feels wrong!
There's a person in here.
A woman...
There's a woman in here!
What are you doing?!

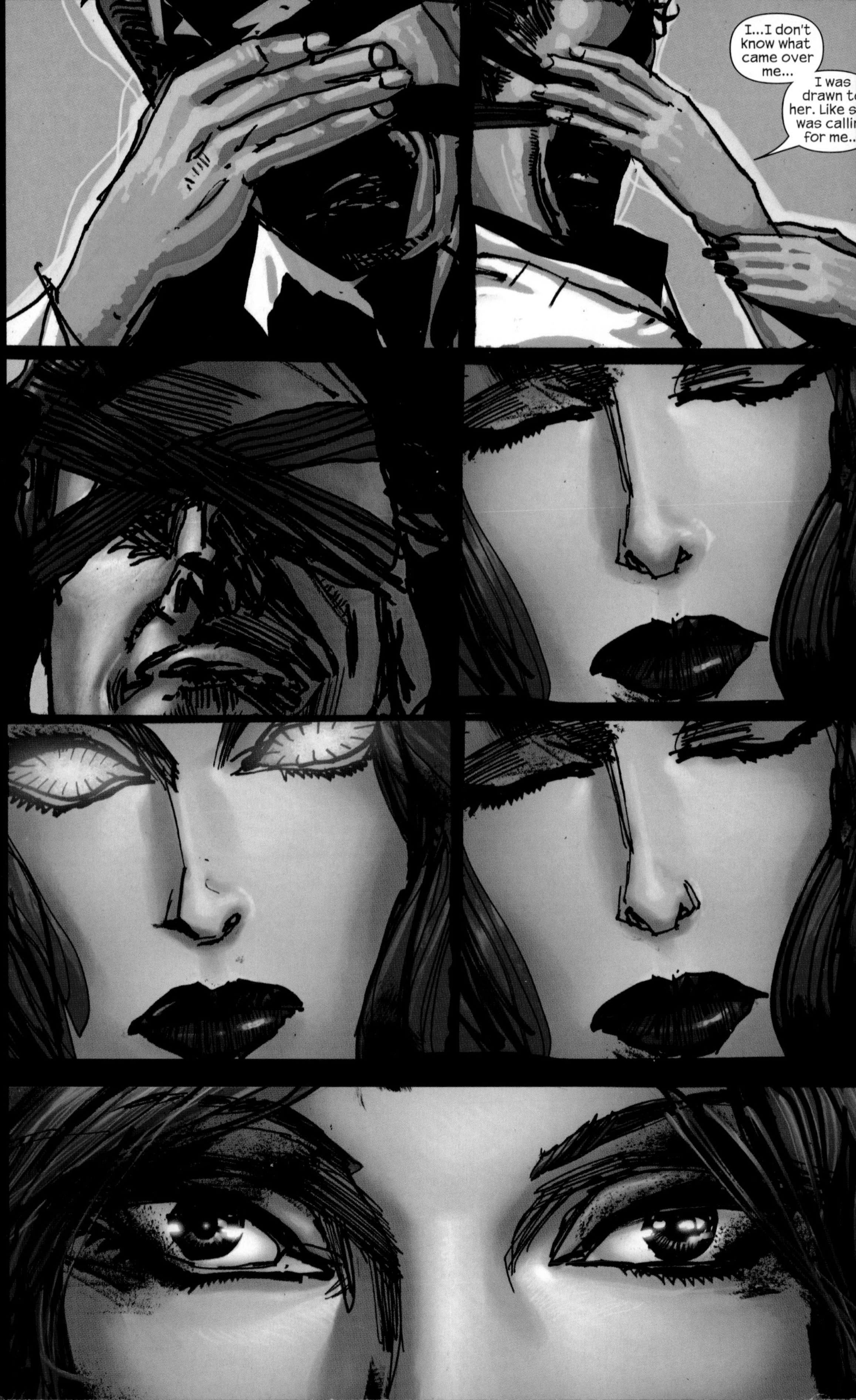
I...I don't know what came over me...
I was drawn t
her. Like s
was callin
for me...

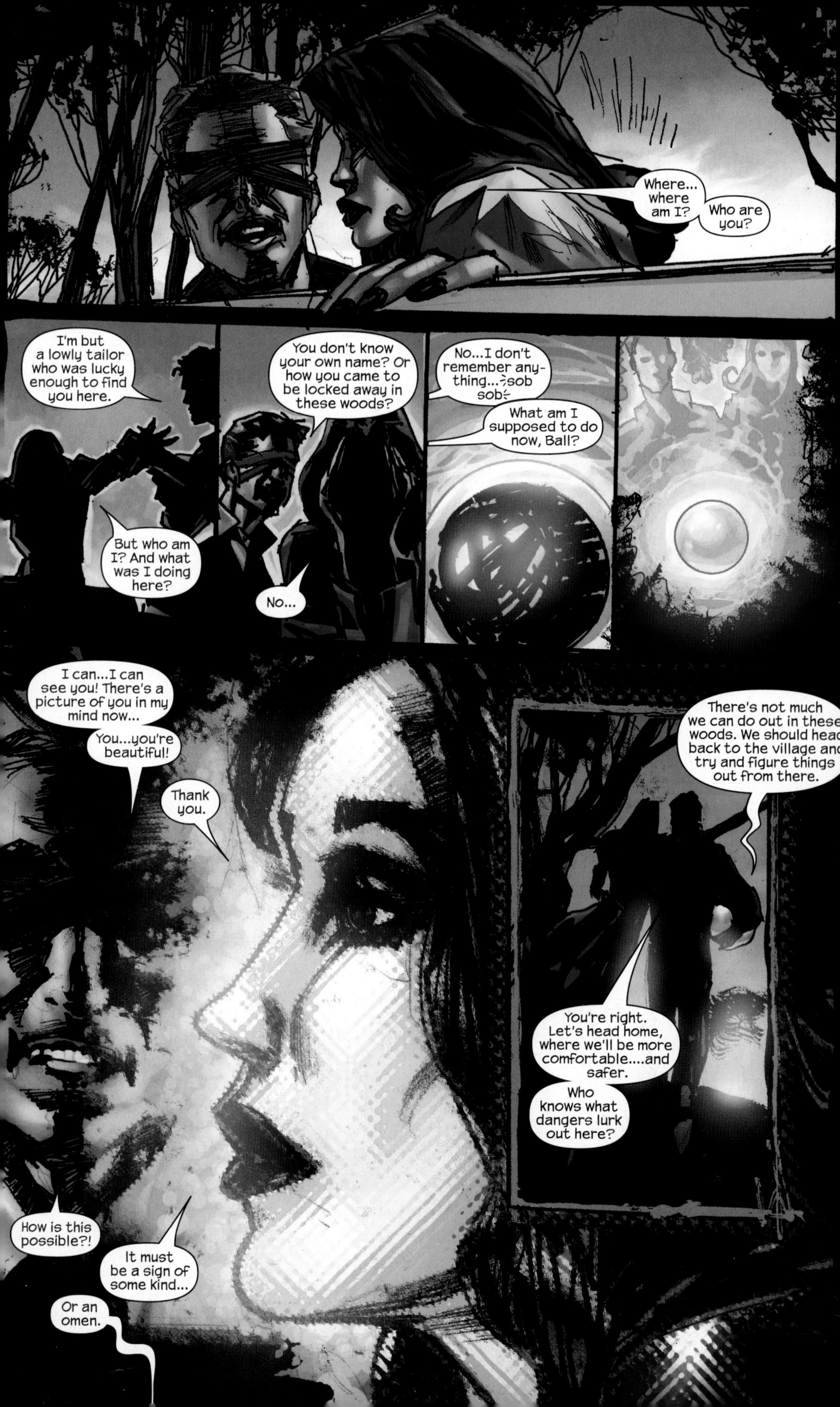
Where... where am I?
Who are you?
I'm but a lowly tailor who was lucky enough to find you here.
But who am I? And what was I doing here?
You don't know your own name? Or how you came to be locked away in these woods?
No...
No...I don't remember any-thing...⩥sob sob⩤
What am I supposed to do now, Ball?
I can...I can see you! There's a picture of you in my mind now...
You...you're beautiful!
Thank you.
How is this possible?!
It must be a sign of some kind...
Or an omen.
There's not much we can do out in these woods. We should head back to the village and try and figure things out from there.
You're right. Let's head home, where we'll be more comfortable....and safer.
Who knows what dangers lurk out here?

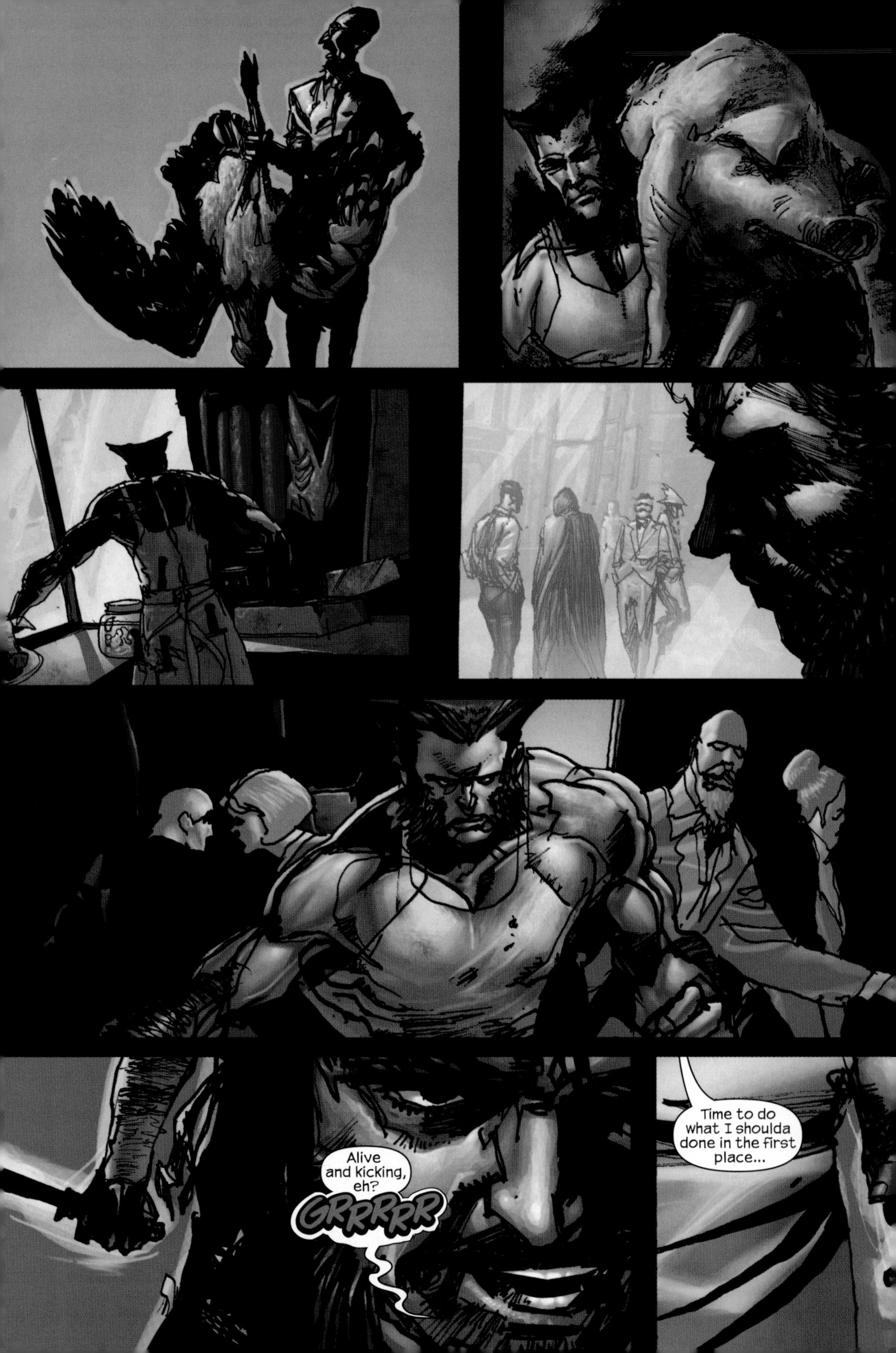
Alive and kicking, eh?
GRRRRR
Time to do what I shoulda done in the first place...

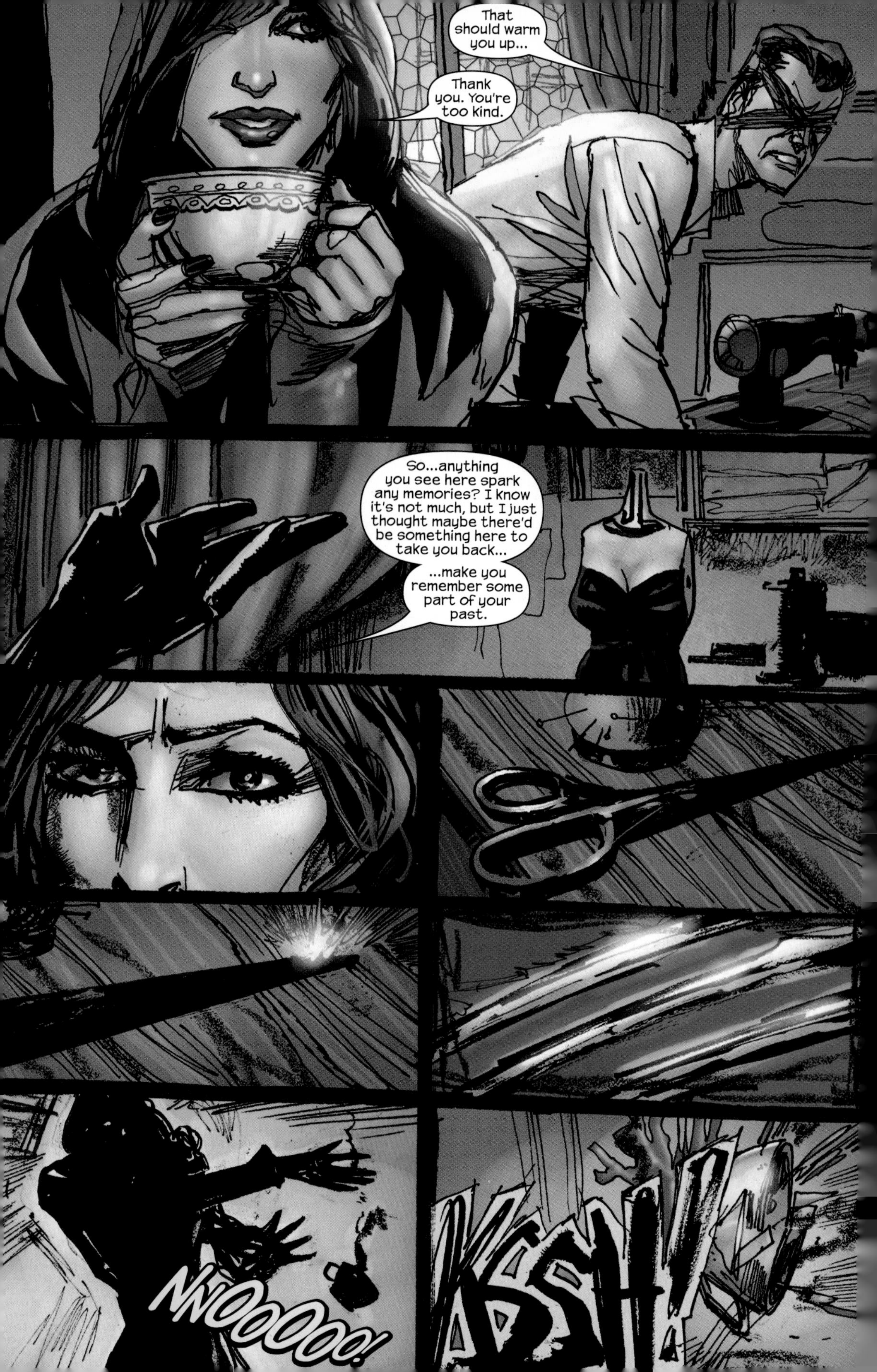
That should warm you up...
Thank you. You're too kind.
So...anything you see here spark any memories? I know it's not much, but I just thought maybe there'd be something here to take you back...
...make you remember some part of your past.
NNOOOOOO!
KSSH!

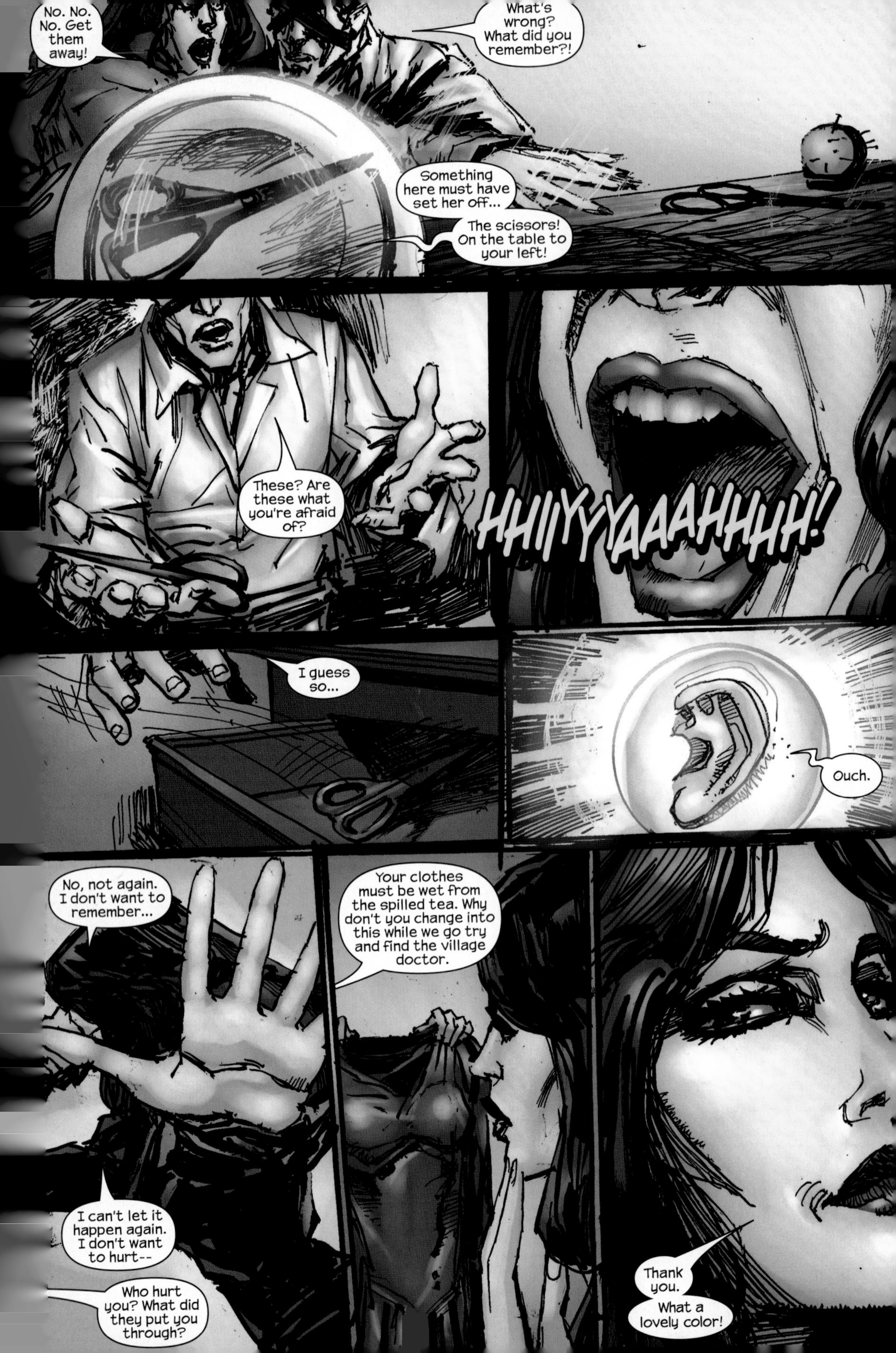
No. No. No. Get them away!
What's wrong? What did you remember?!
Something here must have set her off...
The scissors! On the table to your left!
These? Are these what you're afraid of?
HHIIYYAAAHHHH!
I guess so...
Ouch.
No, not again. I don't want to remember...
I can't let it happen again. I don't want to hurt--
Who hurt you? What did they put you through?
Your clothes must be wet from the spilled tea. Why don't you change into this while we go try and find the village doctor.
Thank you.
What a lovely color!

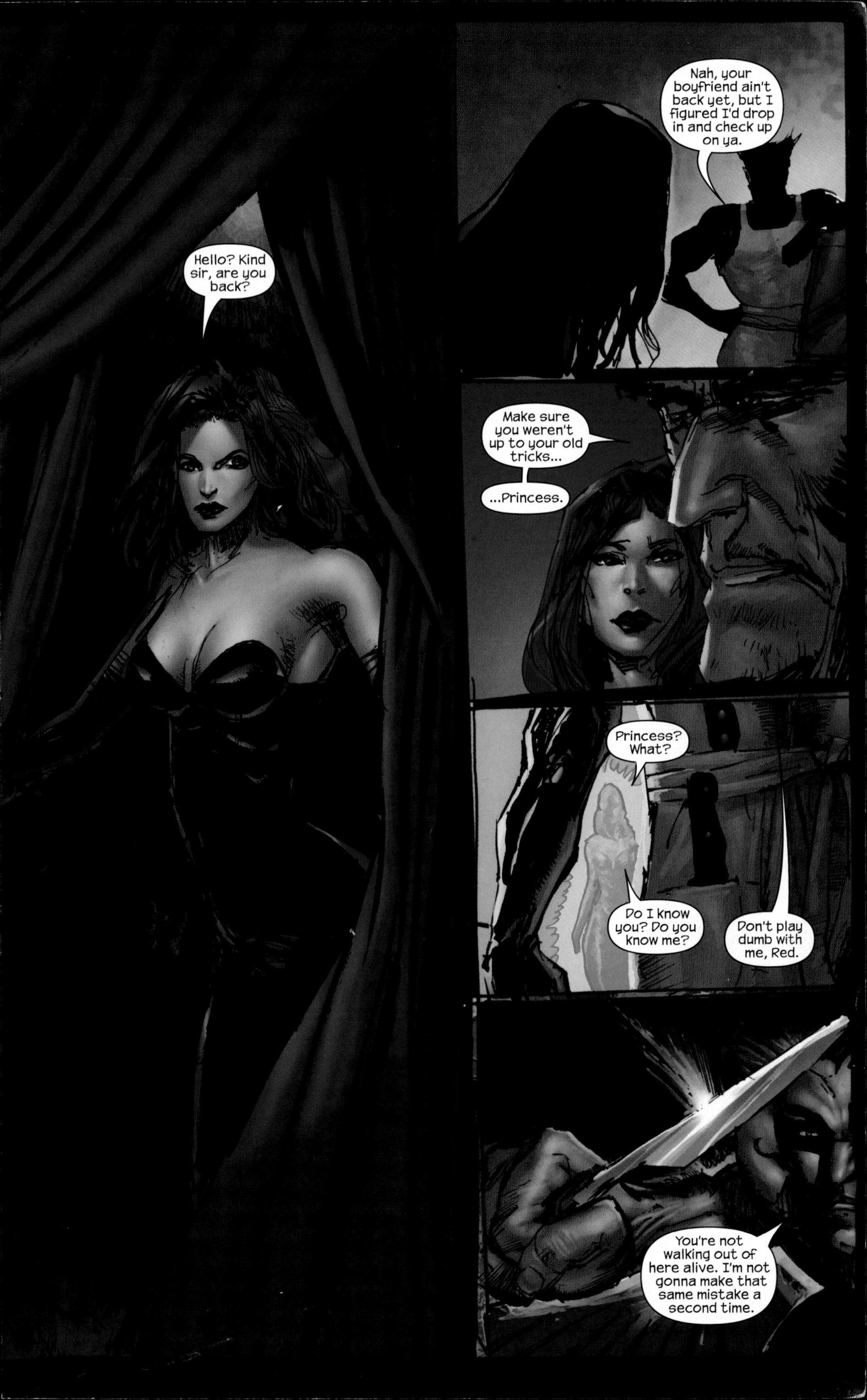
Hello? Kind sir, are you back?
Nah, your boyfriend ain't back yet, but I figured I'd drop in and check up on ya.
Make sure you weren't up to your old tricks...
...Princess.
Princess? What?
Do I know you? Do you know me?
Don't play dumb with me, Red.
You're not walking out of here alive. I'm not gonna make that same mistake a second time.

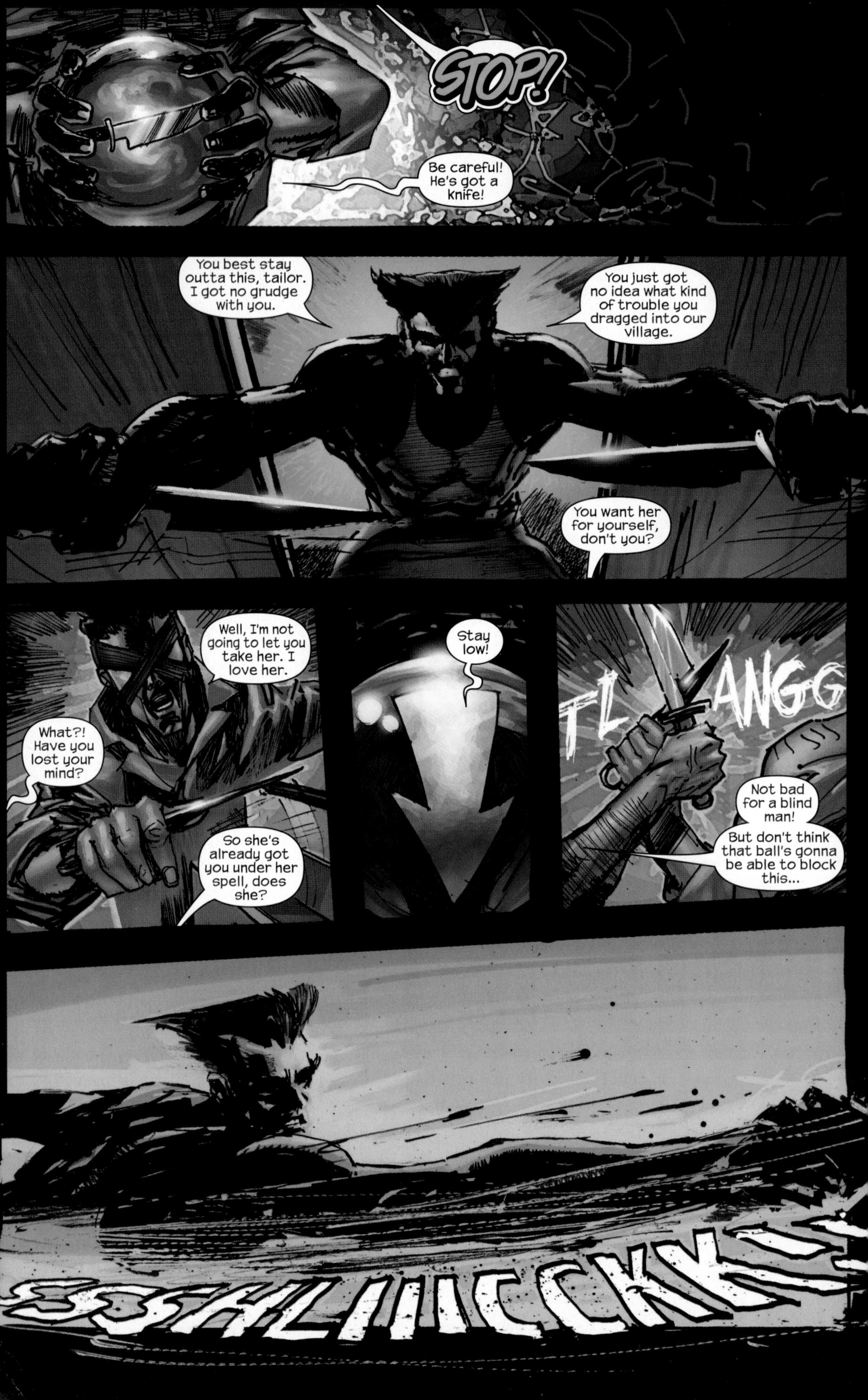
STOP!
Be careful! He's got a knife!
You best stay outta this, tailor. I got no grudge with you.
You just got no idea what kind of trouble you dragged into our village.
You want her for yourself, don't you?
Well, I'm not going to let you take her. I love her.
What?! Have you lost your mind?
So she's already got you under her spell, does she?
Stay low!
TLANGG
Not bad for a blind man!
But don't think that ball's gonna be able to block this...
SSHLIIICCKK

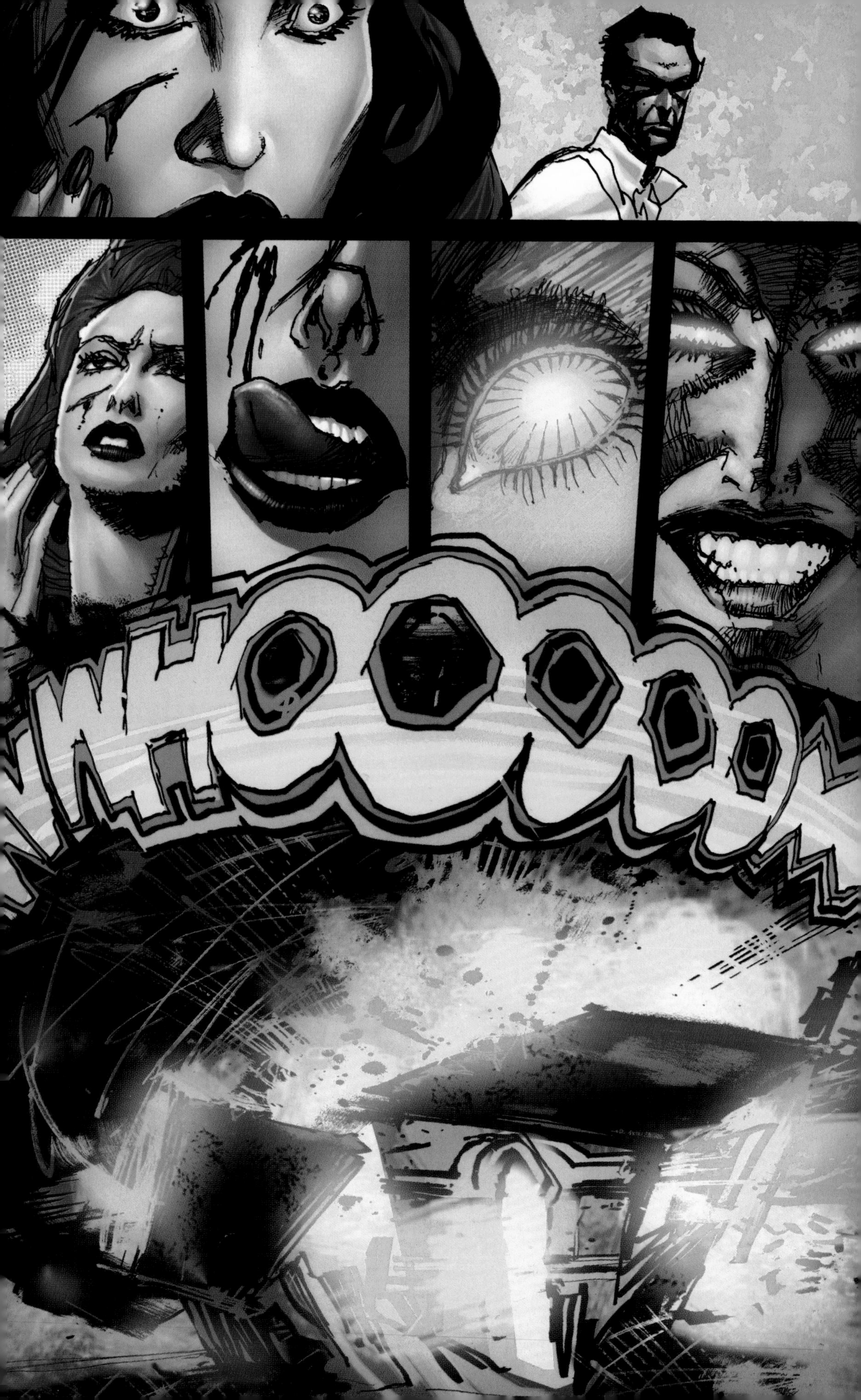
WHOOOOO

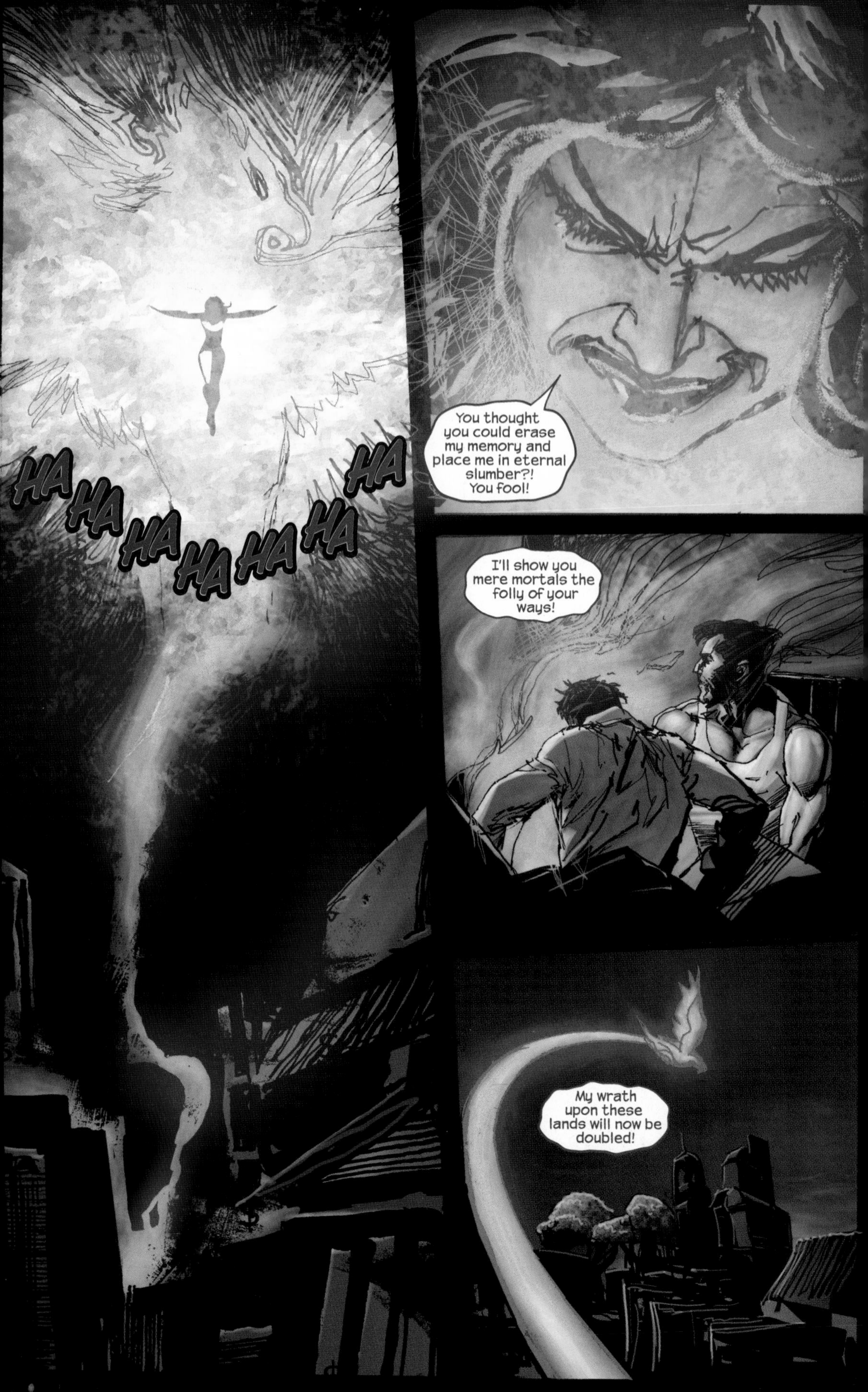
HA HA HA HA HA HA HA
You thought you could erase my memory and place me in eternal slumber?! You fool!
I'll show you mere mortals the folly of your ways!
My wrath upon these lands will now be doubled!

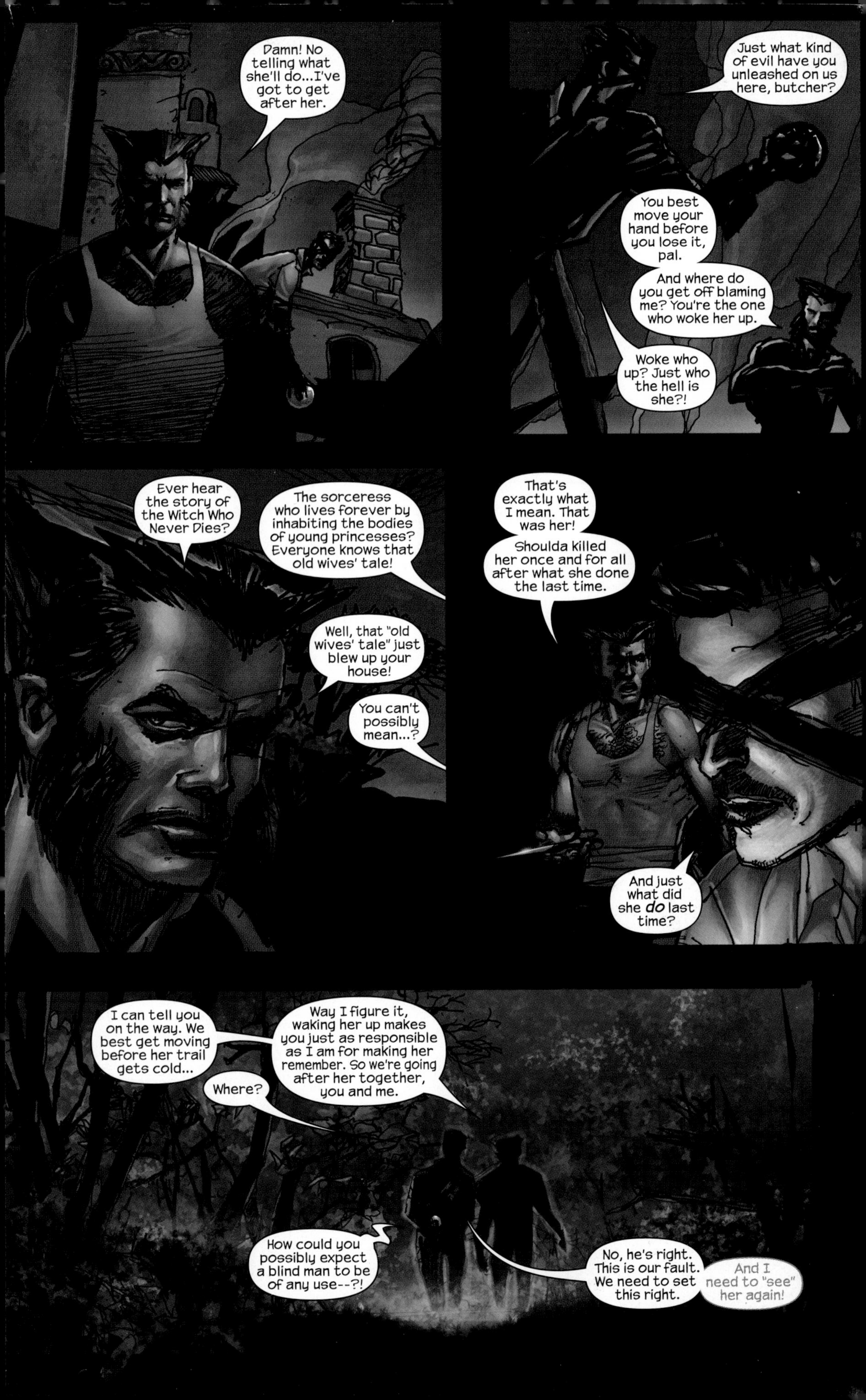
Damn! No telling what she'll do...I've got to get after her.
Just what kind of evil have you unleashed on us here, butcher?
You best move your hand before you lose it, pal.
And where do you get off blaming me? You're the one who woke her up.
Woke who up? Just who the hell is she?!
Ever hear the story of the Witch Who Never Dies?
The sorceress who lives forever by inhabiting the bodies of young princesses? Everyone knows that old wives' tale!
Well, that "old wives' tale" just blew up your house!
You can't possibly mean...?
That's exactly what I mean. That was her!
Shoulda killed her once and for all after what she done the last time.
And just what did she *do* last time?
I can tell you on the way. We best get moving before her trail gets cold...
Where?
Way I figure it, waking her up makes you just as responsible as I am for making her remember. So we're going after her together, you and me.
How could you possibly expect a blind man to be of any use--?!
No, he's right. This is our fault. We need to set this right.
And I need to "see" her again!

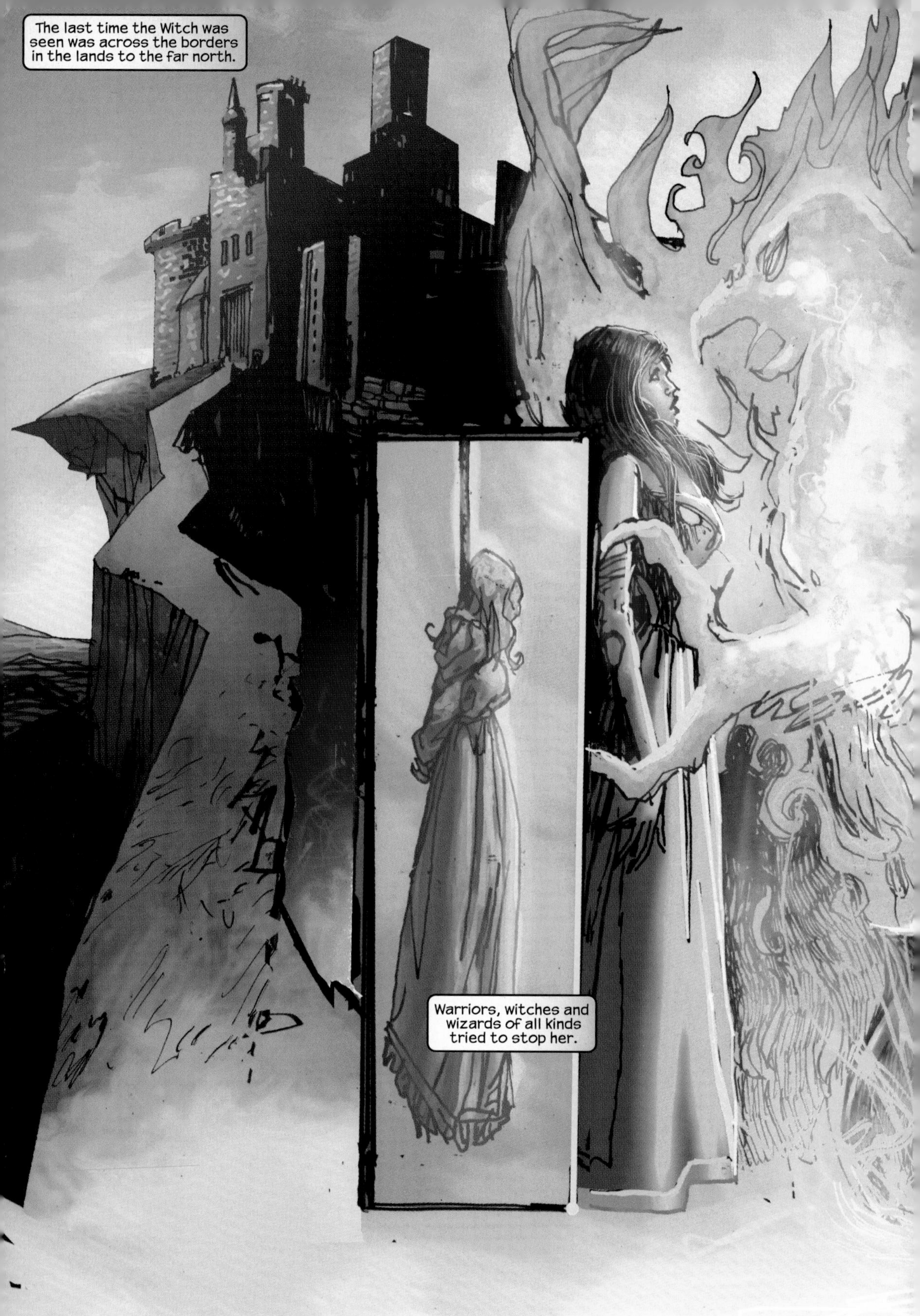
The last time the Witch was seen was across the borders in the lands to the far north.
Warriors, witches and wizards of all kinds tried to stop her.

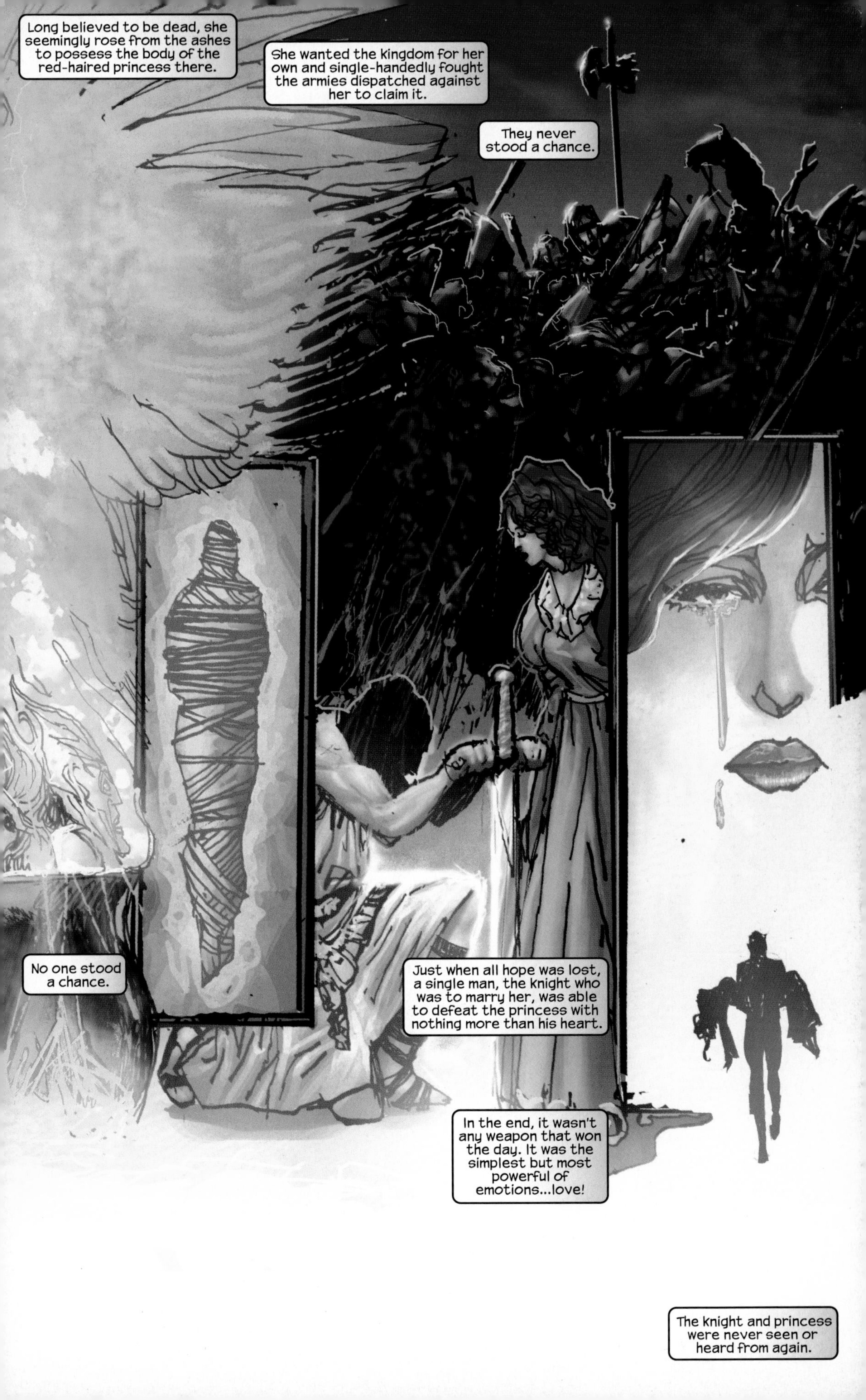
Long believed to be dead, she seemingly rose from the ashes to possess the body of the red-haired princess there.
She wanted the kingdom for her own and single-handedly fought the armies dispatched against her to claim it.
They never stood a chance.
No one stood a chance.
Just when all hope was lost, a single man, the knight who was to marry her, was able to defeat the princess with nothing more than his heart.
In the end, it wasn't any weapon that won the day. It was the simplest but most powerful of emotions...love!
The knight and princess were never seen or heard from again.

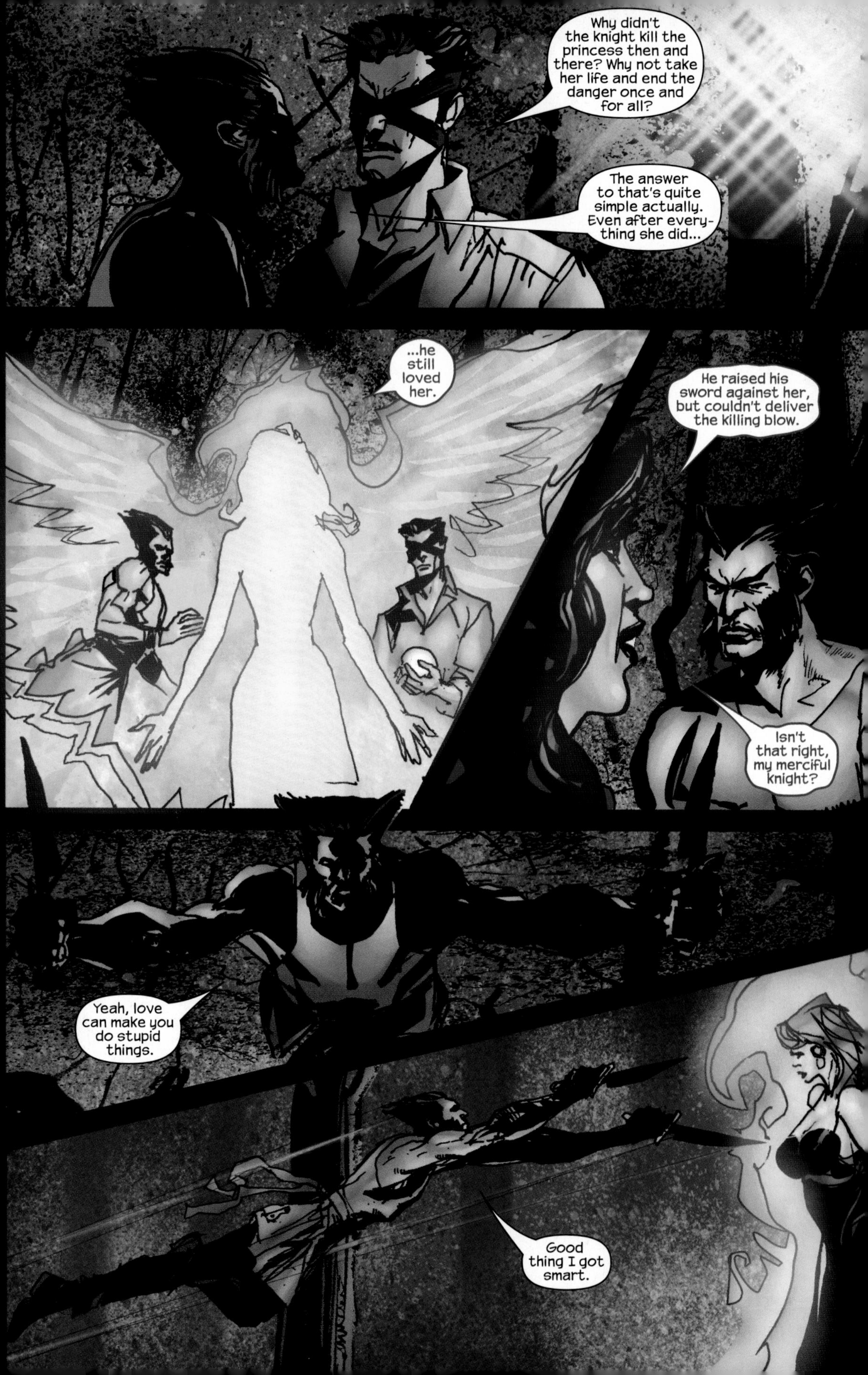
Why didn't the knight kill the princess then and there? Why not take her life and end the danger once and for all?
The answer to that's quite simple actually. Even after every-thing she did...
...he still loved her.
He raised his sword against her, but couldn't deliver the killing blow.
Isn't that right, my merciful knight?
Yeah, love can make you do stupid things.
Good thing I got smart.

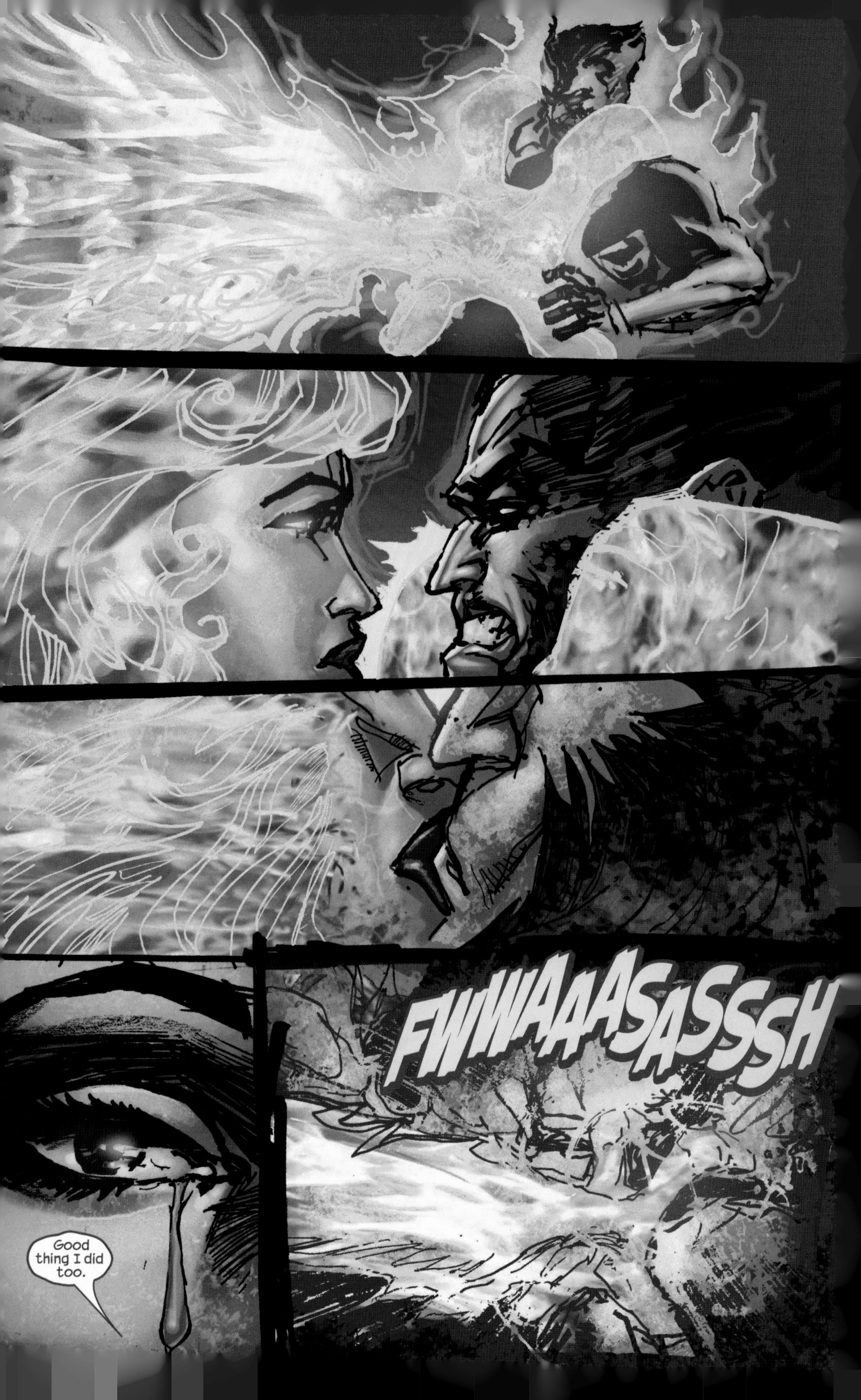
FWWAAASASSSH
Good thing I did too.

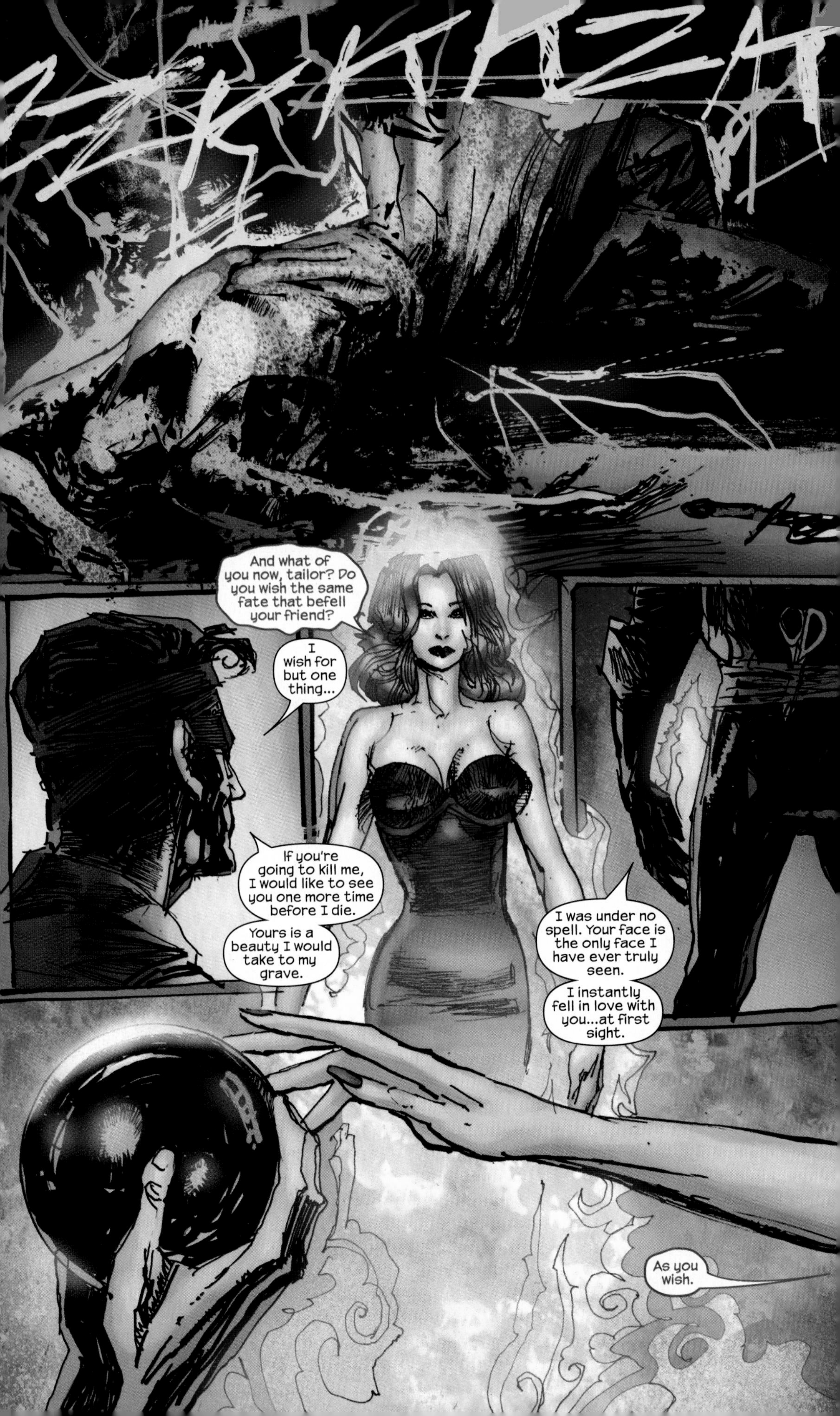
ZZKKTHZAT
And what of you now, tailor? Do you wish the same fate that befell your friend?
I wish for but one thing...
If you're going to kill me, I would like to see you one more time before I die.
Yours is a beauty I would take to my grave.
I was under no spell. Your face is the only face I have ever truly seen.
I instantly fell in love with you...at first sight.
As you wish.

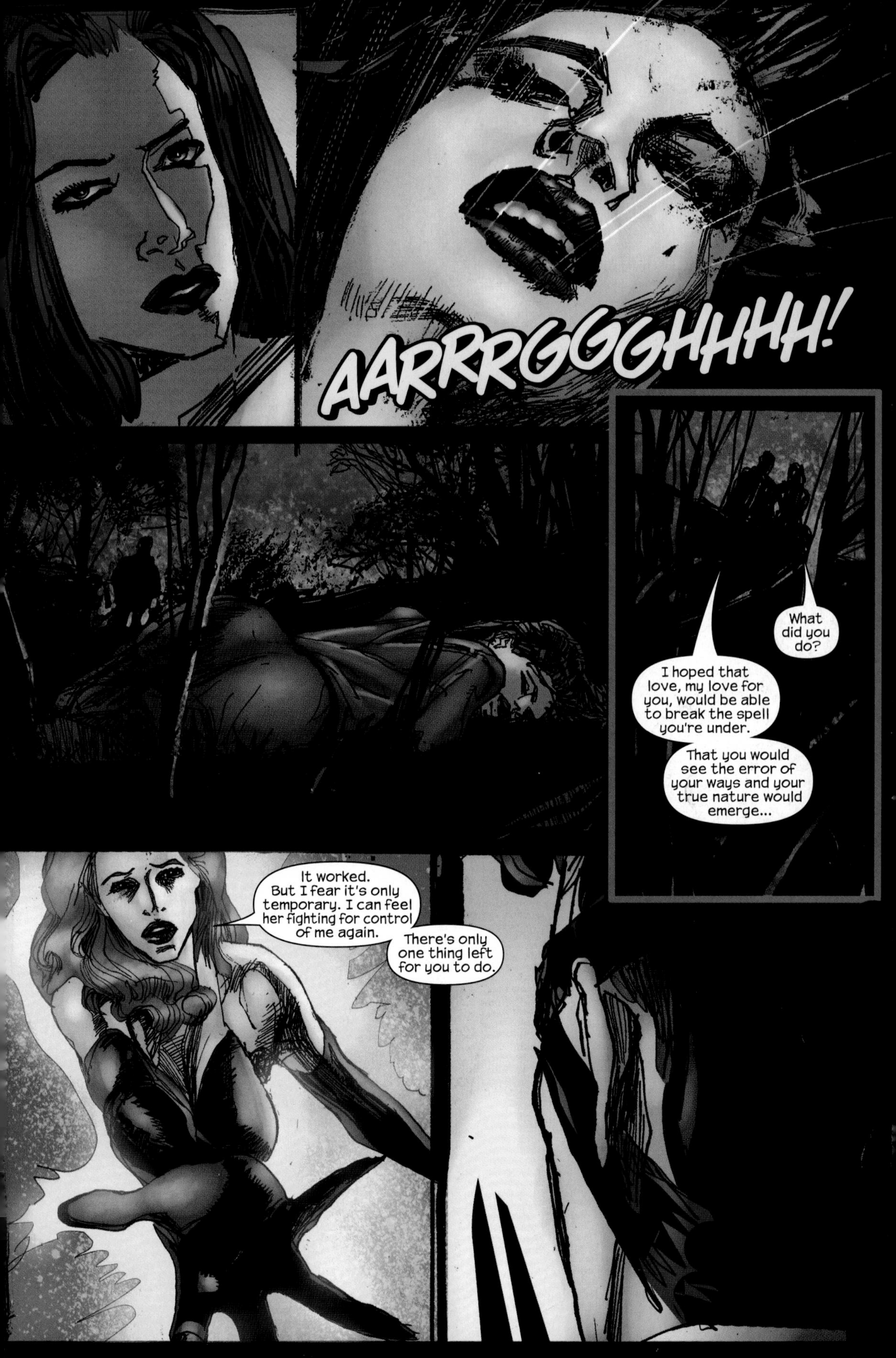
AARRRGGGHHHH!
What did you do?
I hoped that love, my love for you, would be able to break the spell you're under.
That you would see the error of your ways and your true nature would emerge...
It worked. But I fear it's only temporary. I can feel her fighting for control of me again.
There's only one thing left for you to do.

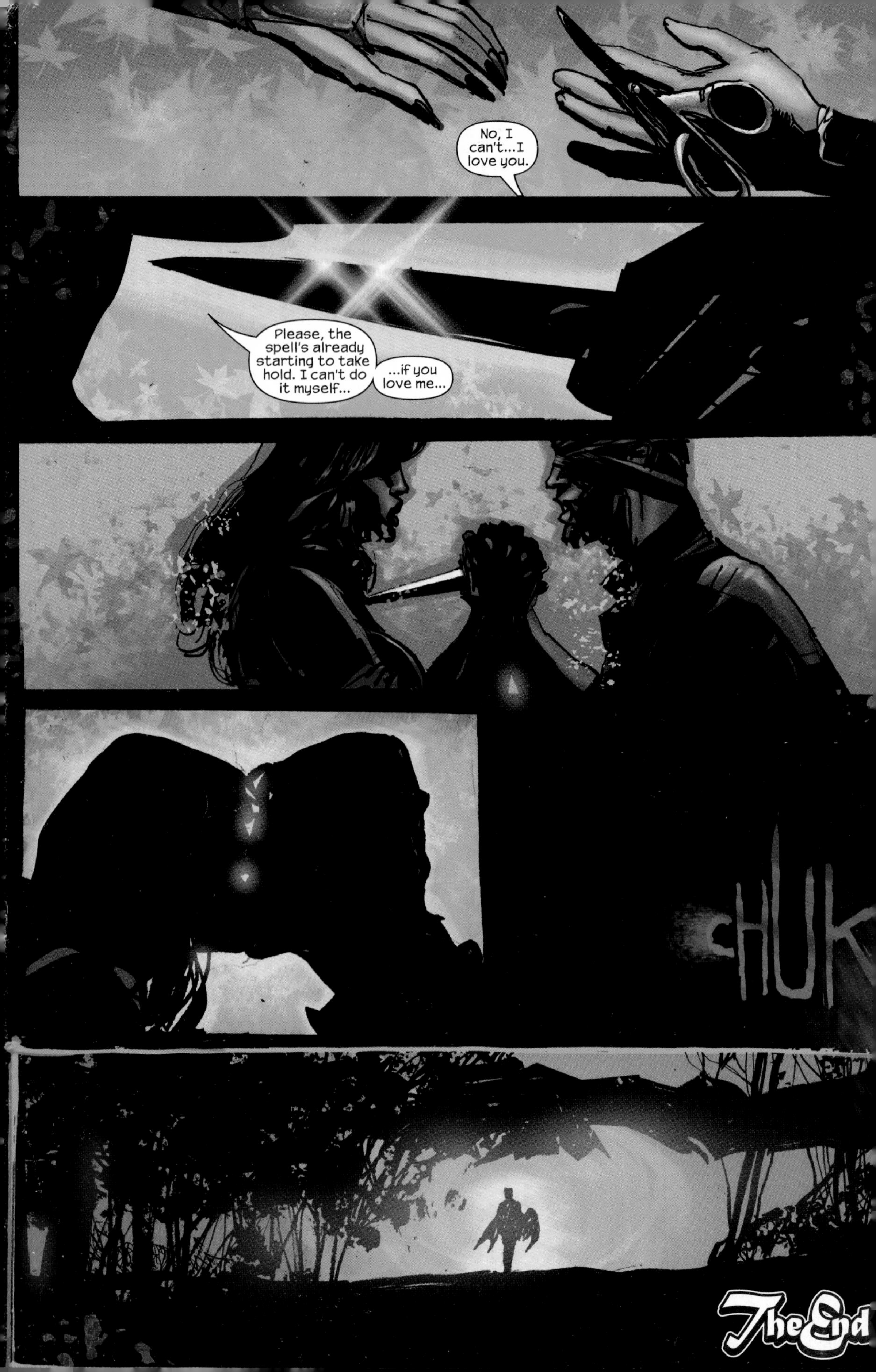
No, I can't...I love you.
Please, the spell's already starting to take hold. I can't do it myself...
...if you love me...
CHUK
The End